Dedication

To Joe, Wynn, Shannon, and Allison

Acknowledgments

Many thanks to Jenny Youngman,
Tony Peterson, Joy Thompson,
and the kind folks at Abingdon.
Thanks also to the youth and the staff
at University Heights United Methodist Church.

LAST-
MINUTE
MEETINGS:

101 Ready-to-Go
Games & Lessons
for Busy Youth Leaders

LAST-MINUTE MEETINGS:

101 Ready-to-Go Games & Lessons for Busy Youth Leaders

Todd Outcalt

Abingdon Press
Nashville

LAST-MINUTE MEETINGS:
101 READY-TO-GO GAMES & LESSONS FOR BUSY YOUTH LEADERS

Copyright © 2001 by Abingdon Press.

This book is printed on acid-free, recycled paper.

Library of Congress Cataloging-in-Publication Data

Outcalt, Todd.
   Last-minute meetings : 101 ready-to-go games & lessons for busy youth leaders / by Todd Outcalt.
      p. cm. — (Essentials for Christian youth)
   ISBN 0-687-09936-6 (pbk. : alk. paper)
   1. Church group work with youth. I. Title. II. Series.

BV4446.O97 2001
268'.433—dc21

                                                                    2001022316

Unless otherwise noted, Scripture quotations are from the *New Revised Standard Version of the Bible,* copyright © 1989, Divison of Christian Education of the National Council of the Churches of Christ in the United States of America. Used by permission. All rights reserved.

01 02 03 04 05 06 07 08 09 10—10 9 8 7 6 5 4 3 2 1

MANUFACTURED IN THE UNITED STATES OF AMERICA

Contents

Introduction

Being a youth leader can be tough. Sometimes preparing for youth meetings takes a back seat to other ministry needs or family concerns. Sometimes a guest speaker doesn't show. Perhaps a key volunteer comes down with the flu. And there are meetings when the best-laid plans go awry at the last minute and you have to whip up a new plan on the spot.

That's why this book was created. Every youth leader needs a resource filled with quick, easy-to-use ideas that can transform a potentially stressful situation into a powerful youth meeting.

In this book, you will find a wealth of ideas that you can use with ease, but also with confidence. Included are Bible lessons, discussions, challenging quizzes, and a wide variety of copy-ready handouts for any situation. You will also find entertaining games that require little or no setup, and a variety of inspiring talks. No matter how you use this resource, LAST-MINUTE MEETINGS is sure to be a big hit with youth and an even bigger hit for you.

Chapter 1

Games at a Glance

What youth leader has not, from time to time, wanted a few quick games to fill time or to rescue a busy week? Here are some games that can be enjoyed with little or no preparation or props. Circle games, relays, group games--a bit of everything can be found here. Use these games when you need them most--as a last-minute rescue!

What's Missing?

Give the youth five minutes to study the environs of the meeting room. Then ask them to step out of the room. After they leave, remove one item (for example: lamp, book, picture) and place it out of sight. Call the youth back into the room and have them guess what's missing. The first person to identify the missing item gets to stay in the room and remove the next item. Other ways to play this game involve (1) removing an item from a person and (2) placing several dozen items in a large pile in the center of the room. Remove an item from the individual or the pile to play.

Give Me Ten

Allow everyone to study an older ten-dollar bill for two minutes (front and back). With larger groups, you may need several ten-dollar bills to distribute to smaller teams. After two minutes, collect the paper money and ask these questions:

💲 Whose image is on the front of the ten-dollar bill? (Alexander Hamilton)

🏛 What building is shown on the back of the bill? (US Treasury)

⊕ How many cars can be seen on the back of the bill? (4)

⚜ How many flags can be seen on the back of the bill? (2)

💲 How many statues can be seen on the back of the bill? (1)

🔟 How many times does the word *Ten* appear on the front of the bill? (6)

❁ What city is written on the front of the bill, right side? (Washington, DC)

🐚 What words appear at the very top of the bill? (Federal Reserve Note)

◯ What color is Hamilton's shirt? (white)

♰ How many times is "In God We Trust" written on the bill? (1)

 # Photographic Memory

To play this game, provide a photograph (a group picture will do nicely). Allow the youth to study the photo for two minutes. Remove the photo, then ask questions such as the following. (Make up other questions to fit your individual photo.)

- How many people were in the photo?

- What color shirt was _____ wearing?

- What color was the wall/background?

- How many clouds were in the sky?

- Who was standing on the far left? far right? in front?

The Name Game

Give each participant a piece of paper and a pencil. Invite each person to write his or her full name (first, middle, last) in the upper corner. The object of the game is to see who can create the most new words using only the letters in his or her name. A letter may not be used more than once. For example, someone named James could create words like *am, me, jam,* and *same,* but not words like *seem, mess,* or *mass.*

Allow five to ten minutes for this game. When the time is up, see who was able to create the most words.

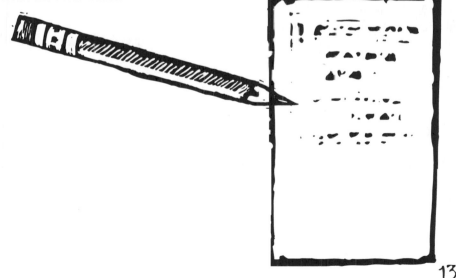

13

Blindfolded Shoe Race

You will need a few blindfolds for this game, and a large, safe area. Invite all the youth to take off their shoes and toss them into a big pile. Untie all the shoes and thoroughly mix them up. Blindfold two or three persons and have them sit down near the edge of the shoe pile. When you say "Go," each blindfolded participant will attempt to find his or her shoes in the assortment. The first person to find his or her shoes, put them on, and tie them, wins that heat. Continue playing until you have a champion.

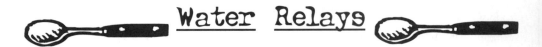

Water Relays

If you are short on time but have access to a kitchen area and utensils, you can create a few quick water game relays with simple, household items. Here are three creative water relays you can play on a moment's notice:

Paper Cup Relay

Fill up two equal-sized pitchers (or large pots) with water. Give each team a paper cup. Each team must transport the water in their container, cup by cup, into another pitcher or pot on the other side of the room.

Spoon Relay

Give each youth a tablespoon and each team a container of water. At the signal, each team must fill a cup on the other side of the room with water, one tablespoon at a time. Each participant has to hold the handle of the tablespoon of water in his or her mouth. When the time is up, the team whose cup holds the most water wins.

Water Hats

Give each person on a team a paper cup full of water. Each team member must balance the cup of water on top of his or her head (without the use of hands) and transport it to the other side of the room. The team that is able to transport the most water in this manner, within the time limit, wins.

Newspaper Editors

Grab a stack of newspapers or magazines, paper, tape, and scissors. Form small teams. Allow 10–15 minutes for each team to create a strange news story by cutting out actual headlines, words, or phrases, and taping them on the paper to form a new article. These creations can be funny or poignant. After hearing each team's news story, talk about whose was the wittiest, the oddest, or the most original.

Pillow Pass

For this game, you will need two pillows of different shapes or colors. Gather the group into a circle and start the game by passing one of the pillows clockwise around the circle. Once everyone has become proficient at passing one pillow, introduce the second pillow into the circle, again passing clockwise.

Here is where the game begins. Whenever the two pillows meet, the person who touches both pillows at the same time must leave the circle. Continue until only three persons remain, then begin again.

 # Toilet Paper Costumes

One last-minute game that is always a hit involves making toilet-paper costumes. You should be able to locate a few rolls of toilet tissue somewhere on short notice. Form teams. Give each team a roll of paper.

Invite the teams to create their own costume presentation by wrapping one team member in the toilet paper. When the teams have finished, vote to see who created the most original, the best-looking, or the funniest presentation.

Dream Team

Form two equal teams and give each team paper and a pencil. See which team has the most points, based on the following system:

1. Award 1 point for each shoelace.

2. Award 2 points for each button.

3. Award 3 points for each white sock.

4. Award 4 points for each zipper.

5. Award 5 points for each necklace.

6. Award 6 points for each *set* of earrings.

7. Award 7 points for each *black* belt.

8. Award 8 points for each *outy* belly button.

9. Award 9 points for each moustache.

10. Award 10 points for each *pinkie* ring.

Mannequin

Form two teams. Tell each group to select one person whom they will "dress up" like a mannequin to earn points. Give the youth 5 to 10 minutes to complete this "dress-up" game. The "mannequins" should be selected with an eye as to who can yield the most points (male/female, fingernails/beard, and so on). Each team earns the following points for having these items on their mannequin when time is called:

1. Earn 1 point if your mannequin has a belt.

2. Earn 2 points if your mannequin has earrings.

3. Earn 3 points if your mannequin has sunglasses (or glasses).

4. Earn 4 points if your mannequin is wearing 4 rings.

5. Earn 5 points if your mannequin is wearing 3 necklaces.

6. Earn 6 points if your mannequin is wearing two watches.

7. Earn 7 points if your mannequin is wearing unmatching socks and shoes.

8. Earn 8 points if your mannequin has a full beard.

9. Earn 9 points if your mannequin is wearing a hat.

10. Earn 10 points if your mannequin has all 10 fingernails painted.

11. Earn 11 points if your mannequin is wearing lipstick.

12. Earn 12 points if your mannequin has a nose ring.

The Buck Stops Here

If you are running short on time but not on cash, try this fun and easy game using a one-dollar bill. Invite the group to leave the meeting room for one minute. Hide the dollar bill somewhere in the room. When the participants return, invite everyone to search for the hidden dollar bill. If you like, allow the lucky person who finds the dollar to keep it as a prize. If you are short on both time and cash, repeat the game by inviting the person who found the buck to hide it a second time. Money always interests youth, and this simple game will provide some guaranteed excitement.

Find the What?

This game can be organized as a relay, or as a game with everyone participating on an individual basis. For larger groups, choose the relay format. For smaller groups, let everyone participate at the same time.

The game begins with the youth leader announcing an object to be found (for example, "Find the paper clip!" or "Find the blue Ping-Pong® paddle!"). The more obscure the object, the longer it will likely take for that object to be located. Whoever locates the item must then bring it back to the leader. This person gets to choose the next object, and the game continues each round in this fashion.

Masking-Tape Sculptures

Form teams of 3–4. Give each team a roll of masking tape. Challenge the groups to construct the best sculpture they can, using the tape. If you like, give each team a few toothpicks to help add texture or support to their work.

The Envelope, Please

Provide business-size envelopes, index cards, and pencils for this game. Form two teams and give each team ten cards and an envelope. Each team must write down an action on each card that they will dare the other team to perform. These actions, however, must not be impossible or vulgar, just funny or challenging.

For example, one card might read: "Everyone must stand on his or her head with feet touching in the middle like a tepee." Another card might read: "Someone in the group must croak like a frog while everyone else hops around the room."

After all ten cards have been completed, each team must place their cards inside the envelope and exchange them with the other team. The teams will then take turns pulling a card from their envelope and trying to perform the actions described there. The team that does the "best job" or is able to perform the most acts can be declared the winner.

Human Hamburgers

For this game you will need several pillows (at least 4; sofa cushions work best); an assortment of posterboard in different colors; and scissors.

Form two teams and give each team several sheets of posterboard. The object of the game is for each team to construct a giant hamburger. The pillows or sofa cushions will be the top and bottom buns; one or two persons will serve as the hamburger patty in the middle; and the posterboard can be cut to look like cheese, pickles, or any other type of hamburger fixings.

Decide on a time limit, and see which team can assemble the best-looking human hamburger.

Human Car Wash

This is a fun game to play outdoors on a hot day, preferably at a pool or a beach, where water is readily available. Provide an assortment of small plastic buckets, some tearless shampoo, and towels. The group members will face one another in two parallel lines, with one person walking down the middle.

As each person proceeds through the "car wash," the other youth will toss water on him or her, then a bucket of tear-free soapy water, then more plain water to rinse off, and finally he or she grabs a towel at the end of the line to dry off. After each person goes through the "car wash," he or she is to grab a bucket and get in line. This is a good cool-down game, but it can also be used on a summer retreat or at a pool party when people are getting bored or you have some time to kill.

Feet Relay

Supply several fairly small objects for this relay game. Round objects such as balls work well, but are more difficult to pass. Soft, pliable objects (pillows, for example) are the easiest to pass.

Form two teams. Have each team's members lie side by side on the floor, face up, to form a line. The object of the relay is to see which team can pass the objects down the line, using only their feet, in the shortest amount of time. The teams can compete simultaneously, or by using a stopwatch, to complete the relay.

 # Feet Meet

Form two teams to play another quick and easy game involving feet. Have each person take off his or her shoes and socks. Then award points based on the following scale. Use a tape measure or yardstick to help tally the results. The team with the most points wins the Feet Meet.

1. 4 points to the team with the largest shoe (by size).

2. 3 points to the team with the smallest shoe (by size).

3. 6 points to the team whose feet, when measured, yield the greatest number of inches.

4. 5 points to the team with the most foot injuries (sprains, blisters, and so on).

5. 7 points to the team with the most white socks.

6. 9 points to the team with the most tennis shoes of one particular brand.

7. 12 points to the team with the most holes in their socks.

8. 15 points to the team with the most painted toenails.

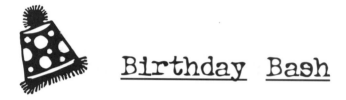 # Birthday Bash

Form two or more teams. Assign points based on the following scale:

1. 3 points to the team with the most people born in January.

2. 4 points to the team with the most people born in April.

3. 5 points to the team with the most people born in the same month.

4. 6 points to any team with someone born on February 28.

5. 7 points to any team with someone born on December 25.

6. 8 points to any team with someone who has a twin.

7. 9 points to any team that includes a person with the same birthday as a parent.

8. 12 points to any team that has someone born on July 4.

9. 15 points to the team that is the oldest (add up the ages of the team members).

10. 20 points to any team that has someone born on a Leap day.

Shoe Shapeup

Form 2–4 teams and have all the team members remove their shoes. Challenge the teams to see who can build the highest structure using only the shoes.

This game looks easier than it is. Set a time limit. Whichever team has the tallest structure when time runs out is the winner.

Penny Pinchers

For this game you will need a few hundred pennies and a small assortment of other pocket change. Gather the youth in a circle and give each person an equal number of coins. If you have a large group, form teams of 8–10 youth. Proceed with the game according to these rules, read aloud in order:

1. Place all your coins face up.

2. Pass all your coins minted before 1950 to the person on your left.

3. Pass all your wheat pennies to the person on your right.

4. Pass all your nickels to the person on your left.

5. Pass all your dimes to the person directly across from you.

6. Pass all your quarters to the person on your right.

7. Pass all coins that have a "D" on them to the person on your left.

8. If you have coins minted in the current year, pass these to the person on your left.

9. If you have coins minted in 1979, pass these coins to the person on your right.

10. Count the number of coins in your possession. The person with the most coins is the winner.

Match-Makers

This is a fun game you can use to mix boys and girls together. You will need index cards and pencils. Give each person an index card and a pencil, then read aloud the following instructions:

1. If you are a male, write a large *M* in the upper right-hand corner of your card. If you are a female, write a large *F* in the upper right-hand corner of your card.

2. Number your card from 1 to 3 and write your name on the back of the card.

3. Fill in your answers to the following questions:

   - Question #1: Which do you choose—Blue or Red?
   - Question #2: Which do you choose—Pepperoni or Sausage?
   - Question #3: Which do you choose—Swim or Go to a Movie?

Use the answers on the cards to form groups. Form card piles with common answers (for example: Blue/Pepperoni/Swim, or Red/Pepperoni/Movie, and so on) and have the youth gather in these groups. These formations may be used for another game, for discussion groups, or as a time to deepen friendships.

Are You Al?

This is a fun icebreaker for a larger group. Before the meeting, secretly assign one of the youth to be "Al." Tell this person to reveal his or her identity only after having spoken to twenty people.

Begin the game by telling the group that someone in the room is named Al. Each group member is to try to discover who Al is. The youth must go from person to person and ask, "Are you Al?" Eventually, Al will say, "Yes, I'm Al." The person who discovers Al wins a prize.

The Number Name Game

Here's another fast and easy game you can organize with minimum time and effort. Supply paper and pencils. Invite everyone to write his or her full name (first, middle, last) at the top of the paper. To play the game, follow these steps, which can be read aloud:

1. Give yourself 1 point for every *e* in your name.

2. Give yourself 2 points for every *u* in your name.

3. Give yourself 3 points for every *r* in your name.

4. Give yourself 4 points if you have more than 6 letters in your first name.

5. Give yourself 5 points if you have more than 8 letters in your last name.

6. Give yourself 6 points if at least two of your names (first/middle/last) begin with the same letter.

7. Give yourself 7 points if any of your names (first/middle/last) rhyme with each other.

8. Give yourself 8 points if your parents named you after someone famous.

9. Give yourself 9 points if you are a junior or you are named after your mother.

10. Give yourself 10 points if you have a biblical name.

The person with the most points rules!

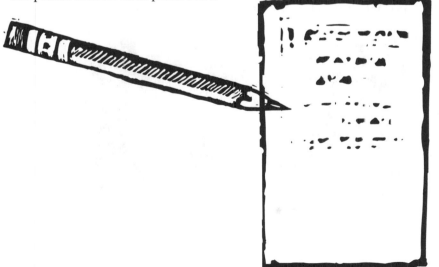

Disk Olympics

Here is an active game you can use outdoors. You'll need a supply of flying disks (Frisbees™). Begin by forming two teams. Give each team a number of disks and ask each team to choose people to participate in the following games. Award a point for each team that loses an event. The team with the lowest score at the end of the Olympics wins.

1. **Disk Toss**—Throwing from behind a line, the person with the longest toss wins.

2. **Disk Catch**—Each participant must toss his or her own disk at least ten feet into the air and then catch it. Whoever can catch the most in a row wins.

3. **Disk Roll**—For this event, participants must roll the disk on the ground. The farthest roll wins.

4. **Disk Spin**—Participants must spin the disk on a finger. The longest-timed spin wins.

5. **Disk Relay**—Teams of two must throw the disk between two points fifty feet apart. The team catching the most in succession without dropping the disk wins.

6. **Disk Run**—Participants (2) must work together to toss and catch a disk. With one person standing behind a line, another must run from a starting point fifty feet away. Whoever catches the most tossed disks in a row wins.

7. **Disk Goal**—Participants must toss a disk into a wastecan positioned ten feet away. Whoever sinks the most tosses out of ten tries, wins.

Chapter 2

Handy Handouts

Here are five timely tips for using these handouts effectively:

(1) Use handouts as discussion-starters. (2) Center a meeting around the topic of a handout. (3) Give everyone a chance to tell his or her opinion related to the subject matter. (4) Use handouts as energy boosts. (5) Use handouts as take-home projects that will get the youth thinking about a particular topic throughout the week.

1

Something About Me

Be prepared to comment on your responses to these statements:

The thing I like most about me is

The one subject or area of interest I know the most about is

Some day I would like to live in

My favorite movie of all time is

I'm at my best when

The person in the Bible with whom I most identify is

My favorite meal is

My favorite musical group is

The most important day of my life was when

The most awesome thing I have ever seen was

From LAST-MINUTE MEETINGS, by Todd Outcalt. © 2001 by Abingdon Press.

Whatever Will Be Will Be?

2

Be prepared to comment on your insights about the future:

The most important decision I have to make tomorrow is

The most important decision I have to make in the next year is

Five years from now I want to be

Ten years from now I want to be

For me, the 3 most helpful methods of making decisions are

(1)

(2)

(3)

When I think about the future, I feel

When I think about *my* future, I feel

I believe God is leading me to

If I could ask for one thing to help me in the future, it would be

What I hope to achieve with my life is

From LAST-MINUTE MEETINGS, by Todd Outcalt. © 2001 by Abingdon Press.

3

Yours Truly

Write a letter to your youth group using the following three questions as a thought-provoking guide. Be prepared to read your letter to the group.

What do you most need from your group?

What do you most want to give to your group?

How have you experienced God's love from your group?

Dear _____:

Yours truly,

From LAST-MINUTE MEETINGS, by Todd Outcalt. © 2001 by Abingdon Press.

The Job Application

Fill out this sample application, then discuss the questions on the following page:

NAME:

ADDRESS: ZIP:

PHONE: SS#:

E-MAIL ADDRESS:

SEX: RACE:

For Our Files

Previous Job Experience:

Educational Background:

Personal Information:

What skills do you bring to this position that might help advance our company?

Have you had any serious health problems in the past five years?

What makes you think you can do this job?

What salary are you looking for in a position such as this?

From LAST-MINUTE MEETINGS, by Todd Outcalt. © 2001 by Abingdon Press.

Questions for Discussion

1. What made completing this job application difficult?

2. Should employers know applicants' race or sex? Why or why not?

3. How much weight do you think should be given to a person's work experience?

4. How much weight should be given to education or to classroom learning?

5. Should employers have access to details about applicants' health?

6. If you were an employer, how might your opinion be different?

7. If you were an employer, what would you want to know about your applicants? How would you propose to get accurate information in ways that would also be fair?

8. What, in your mind, constitutes the perfect workplace?

9. What would a great employer do for you?

10. What should you, as an employee, provide for your employer?

Letter to Myself

6

Take a few minutes to write a letter to yourself, in which you answer the following questions. Your letter can be kept in confidence, or read aloud in a group setting.

What are the greatest challenges I am facing at this stage of my life?

How am I doing?

What hopes do I have for the future?

Dear _____,

Yours truly,

From LAST-MINUTE MEETINGS, by Todd Outcalt. © 2001 by Abingdon Press.

My Prayer List

Use the following outline to organize a prayer list. Make an effort, for one month, to pray for the joys and concerns you have on your list.

People Who Need My Prayers   **Guidance I Am Seeking**

1.   1.

2.   2.

3.   3.

4.   4.

5.   5.

Things I Don't Understand   **People and Things I Need**

1.   1.

2.   2.

3.   3.

Gifts and Blessings for Which I Am Thankful

1.

2.

3.

4.

5.

Note to Leaders: This handout works well with a lesson on prayer. Allow the youth to take home their prayer list, and remind the participants to refer to the list daily.

The Interview

8

Use these questions to interview members of the youth group. You may choose to videotape the interviews, or simply use a live format in a youth meeting.

1. What brings you back to youth meetings?

2. How have you experienced God's love or presence lately?

3. How might your life be different if not for the youth group?

4. What recent youth event or discussion have you enjoyed the most?

5. What keeps you laughing?

6. What keeps you humble?

7. What's the best thing you have done for someone else?

8. What do you hope our group can do for others in the coming year?

9

My Homework Assignment

Use this handy outline to practice your discipleship this week:

Monday

1. Start the week with a positive attitude and a prayer.

2. Do something nice for someone at school (maybe someone who has few friends).

Tuesday

1. Pray for 5 minutes.

2. Help a parent with a chore at home.

Wednesday

1. Read the Bible for 5 minutes.

2. List 3 ways you can improve your life.

Thursday

1. Pray for 10 minutes.

2. Read the Bible for 10 minutes.

Friday

1. Pray for 15 minutes.

2. Invite a friend to church the coming weekend.

Saturday

1. Read the Bible for 15 minutes.

2. Participate in a group project designed to benefit others (a soup kitchen, a mission event, a clothing co-op, and so on).

Career Choices

10

This handout could supplement a career day or a discussion about vocations:

Instructions: Write down your top three career choices. Using the grid below the choices, grade each career (1—very favorable, 3—average, 5—unfavorable). See which career has the greatest advantages/disadvantages (the lowest score denotes the closest match).

Right now, my top three career choices would be:

	1.	2.	3.
Required training/schooling College, graduate school, technical school			
Working conditions Regular or long hours/shift work			
Stability of location Will moves be required?			
Employment outlook Demand increasing or decreasing			
Salary and benefits Starting wage/vacation/retirement			
Satisfaction potential I like this kind of work/not sure			
Fulfillment potential Worthy of my values/worthy of my gifts			
Growth potential Outlook is good/might lead to something else			
TOTAL SCORES			

From LAST-MINUTE MEETINGS, by Todd Outcalt. © 2001 by Abingdon Press.

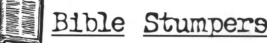 # Bible Stumpers

Use these clues to identify characters in the Bible. If you need extra help, the Answer Key offers a Bible book and chapter related to each clue.

1. I fought the battle of Jericho.

2. I lost everything and lived in the land of Uz.

3. I was second in command under Pharoah, and a child of Jacob.

4. My name means "the grabber."

5. My cousin was a wild man and a baptizer.

6. My husband was Abraham.

7. I was a female judge.

8. I was a prophet who saw Jesus, and was an 84-year-old widow.

9. I sentenced Jesus to die on the cross.

10. I was taken to heaven in a chariot of fire.

11. I was a shepherd boy turned king.

12. My husband, Jacob, worked 7 years and a week to win my hand in marriage.

Answer Key

1. Joshua (Joshua 6)

2. Job (Job 1)

3. Joseph (Genesis 41)

4. Jacob (Genesis 25)

5. Jesus (Luke 1)

6. Sarai/Sarah (Genesis 16–17)

7. Deborah (Judges 4)

8. Anna (Luke 2:36-37)

9. Pontius Pilate (John 19)

10. Elijah (2 Kings 2)

11. David (1 Samuel 16)

12. Rachel (Genesis 29)

Chapter 3

Dynamic Discussions

Good discussions don't have to be dry or super-spiritual. Some of the best involve personal feelings and humor. Here are 17 straightforward discussion-starters that will motivate any youth group . . . even at a moment's notice. The topics may be photocopied for the group, or offered straight out of the book by the youth leader. Either way, your group will get plenty of mileage from these hearty helpers.

Which Would You Choose?

If you had to choose between these options, which would you choose . . . and why?
Would you rather . . .

1. Fail a class . . . or get a speeding ticket?

2. Get turned down for a date . . . or get turned down for a job?

3. Have a scar on your arm . . . or a zit in the middle of your forehead?

4. Make the winning basket for your team . . . or win an academic award?

5. Write a 1000-word essay . . . or give a 10-minute speech?

6. Kiss a pig . . . or kiss a monkey?

7. Have to clean a toilet . . . or do two loads of laundry?

8. Not speak for a day . . . or have no one speak to you for a day?

9. Lose a diamond ring . . . or lose your driver's license?

10. Have to wear braces . . . or eyeglasses?

11. Take a trip to outer space . . . or dive to the bottom of the ocean?

12. Know someone famous . . . or know someone who is rich?

13. Have someone hit you . . . or have someone gossip about you?

14. Wear clothes that are out of style . . . or get a bad haircut?

15. Have a blister on your finger . . . or a splinter in your finger?

From LAST-MINUTE MEETINGS, by Todd Outcalt. © 2001 by Abingdon Press.

Pet Peeves

13

Most people have a pet peeve or two—something that makes them mad or drives them crazy. Which of these comes closest to your personal pet peeve . . . and why? Or if these aren't enough, tell us what your pet peeve is.

1. I can't stand waiting in line . . . when I already have a ticket.

2. I can't stand rude people . . . when everyone else is being nice.

3. I can't stand a boring job . . . when I have other work to do.

4. I can't stand having car trouble . . . when my car is not that old.

5. I can't stand people who are late . . . when everyone else is on time.

6. I can't stand seeing people suffer . . . especially when a solution exists.

7. I can't stand gossip . . . especially when it's unkind.

My pet peeve is _____.

From LAST-MINUTE MEETINGS, by Todd Outcalt. © 2001 by Abingdon Press.

Don't Make Me Laugh

Here are some good discussion-starters that will also provide a few chuckles:

1. What is the funniest thing you have ever seen at school?

2. What is the funniest thing that has happened in your family?

3. What is the best (clean!) joke you have ever heard?

4. Who is the funniest person you know?

5. What funny sounds do you make when you can't stop laughing?

6. Who has the funniest laugh in this room?

7. What is the funniest story you have ever heard?

The Dating Game

This quick discussion-starter builds on teens' strong opinions about dating:

1. From a male perspective . . . what would be a perfect date?

2. From a female perspective . . . what would be a perfect date?

3. Where should a couple go on a first date . . . and why?

4. What are girls really looking for in a guy?

5. What are guys really looking for in a girl?

6. If you had to name a song that would be your song . . . what would it be?

7. Is a group date really a date? Why or why not?

8. What determines if you will go out with a person on a second date?

9. Do you think there is too much emphasis on dating at your school? How so?

10. What's the number one thing you hope to find out about a person on a first date?

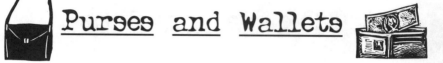

Purses and Wallets

One of the best last-minute discussion-starters involves asking youth to tell what they carry in their purses and wallets. Use these questions to generate some fun:

1. What's the weirdest thing you carry in your purse or wallet?

2. Can you show us the picture of yourself you like the best?

3. Who has the most money in a purse or wallet?

4. What kinds of coupons or receipts do you carry?

5. Whose phone number or address are you carrying?

6. Who has the oldest coin in a purse or wallet?

7. Who has the most pictures in his or her purse or wallet?

From LAST-MINUTE MEETINGS, by Todd Outcalt. © 2001 by Abingdon Press.

Bible Stuff

Just distribute Bibles for these questions; the rest is up to the youth:

1. Read your favorite Bible passage to the group.

2. What is one question you have about the Bible?

3. Which book of the Bible do you think has the strangest name . . . and why?

4. What Bible passage do you find most challenging?

5. What Bible passage do you find most comforting?

From LAST-MINUTE MEETINGS, by Todd Outcalt. © 2001 by Abingdon Press.

Job Hunt

Use this series of questions to generate discussion about the future and careers:

1. What do you regard as the two most important aspects of any job?

2. What do you think makes a good job?

3. What guidelines or standards influence your thinking about a career?

4. What would your perfect job entail?

5. Which is more important in a job: salary or flexibility? Why?

6. If you could work anywhere in the world, where would you go?

7. What would you be willing to sacrifice to get the perfect job?

8. What scares you the most about looking for a permanent job?

9. Who do you think has the best job in the world? Why?

10. Which would you rather do—a job you love, or a job you hate that pays well?

True Friends

1. What qualities make a good friend?

2. Which is more difficult: to have a friend, or to be a friend?

3. Would you rather have lots of friends, or one or two close friends? Why?

4. What would a true friend *not* do?

5. What is the one thing you most enjoy doing with your friends?

6. Do you think people appreciate their friends? Why or why not?

7. How has a friend helped you through a difficult time?

From LAST-MINUTE MEETINGS, by Todd Outcalt. © 2001 by Abingdon Press.

At the Movies

1. What, in your opinion, is the best movie of all time?

2. What makes a good movie?

3. What movie has caused you to think the most?

4. With which movie character do you most closely identify?

5. What is your favorite snack while watching a movie?

6. Can you think of a good movie that others may not have seen? Which one?

7. Can you think of a movie that has brought you closer to God? How?

From LAST-MINUTE MEETINGS, by Todd Outcalt. © 2001 by Abingdon Press.

Listen to the Music

21

1. In your opinion, who is the greatest music group of all time?

2. In your opinion, who is the greatest solo artist of all time?

3. What song has caused you to think the most?

4. Can you think of a song that has brought you closer to God? Which one?

5. If you could choose only one style of music, what would you listen to?

6. If you were on a deserted island with only one CD, which one would you choose? Why?

7. What song would you say is your song? What is the special significance of this song for you?

From LAST-MINUTE MEETINGS, by Todd Outcalt. © 2001 by Abingdon Press.

School Daze

1. What do you enjoy most about school?

2. What do you enjoy least about school?

3. What would make your school a better place for work and study?

4. What is the most important aspect of school?

5. Which teachers have most influenced your life? Why?

6. What events or subjects have most inspired you at school?

7. What do you hope to remember after you graduate?

8. If you were in charge of school for one day, what would you change?

9. What is the most important thing that has happened to you at school?

10. What have you enjoyed most about your school?

Count Your Blessings

23

1. What's the best thing that has happened to you this week?

2. What's the best thing that has happened to you this month?

3. What new opportunities have you experienced lately?

4. When you feel down, what or who lifts you up?

5. How would you describe the blessings in your life?

6. Who has made a difference in your life?

7. In what ways have some difficulties led you closer to God?

8. What challenges have you faced that have turned out to be blessings?

9. What describes the word *blessing*?

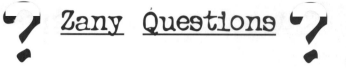

❓ Zany Questions ❓

1. What's the weirdest thing you've ever seen?

2. What's the highest place upon which you've ever stood?

3. What is the strangest-looking car you've ever seen?

4. What's the funniest thing you've seen happen to a complete stranger?

5. Where is the smelliest place you've ever been?

6. What was the worst food you've ever eaten?

7. What is the oddest sound you've ever heard?

8. What is the most mysterious moment you've ever experienced?

9. What is the scariest moment you've ever experienced?

10. What is the strangest question you've ever been asked?

From LAST-MINUTE MEETINGS, by Todd Outcalt. © 2001 by Abingdon Press.

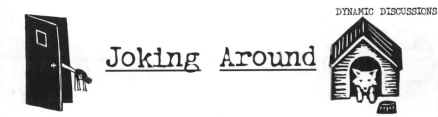

Joking Around

Assign one of the following to each person (or small group). Each person must then recall, or make up, a (clean) joke about that item.

1. A joke about a car

2. A joke about a cat

3. A joke about a dog

4. A joke about forgetfulness

5. A joke about a celebrity

6. A joke about golf

7. A joke concerning an airplane

8. A joke concerning a ship

9. A joke told in a foreign accent

10. A light-bulb joke

From LAST-MINUTE MEETINGS, by Todd Outcalt. © 2001 by Abingdon Press.

Political Potpourri

26

1. What do you think are the most pressing issues for our country?

2. If you were President, what would your platform be?

3. If you were President, whom would you want on your staff?

4. What would you change about politics if you could?

5. If you held elected office, how would you balance your private life and your public life?

6. Do you think people are less interested in politics today than in the past? Why?

7. If you could change one thing about our country, what would you change?

8. Who, currently not running for office, do you think would make a good President?

9. What reforms would you try to bring to the election process?

10. What are some issues that you think politicians try to use to their advantage?

God Stuff 101

1. How would you describe God to someone who has no faith?

2. Why, do you think, does suffering exist in the world?

3. Why, do you think, does God allow suffering?

4. How might suffering be helpful or harmful to our belief in God?

5. What questions do you have about God?

6. What do you find difficult to understand about God?

7. How have you experienced God during the past week?

8. How do you stay close to God?

Note to Leader: The following Scripture passages may help with these deep questions: **Job 42; Psalm 10; Psalm 23; Ecclesiastes 3:1-15; John 9:1-7; John 16:16-24; Revelation 21:1-4.**

What Would Jesus Do?

28

Base your response to the first three situations on your idea of what Jesus would do in each case:

1. For five years you've saved money for college, but you can't decide where to go to school. You have enough to attend a local university, if you continue to live at home. Or you could go to an out-of-state college that has granted you a small scholarship, but end up using all your money in the first year.

2. Your father has a serious illness. You were planning on going to college, and your father wants you to go. But you are torn between staying around home for a year to help your mother, or leaving to pursue a degree.

3. For several months you've been working at a local restaurant on the weekends. A few days ago, you noticed your best friend stealing money from the cash drawer when the manager wasn't looking.

4. Does trying to imagine Jesus' response to certain situations always help us to make decisions? Why or why not?

5. What made the first three situations difficult for you?

6. What spiritual or Christ-centered guidelines help us in making decisions?

7. How might God help us with a complex situation or decision?

Chapter 4

Quick Quizzes

Think a quiz has to be dry or boring? Let the youth decide. After they take these exciting quizzes, you'll have them talking and thinking like never before. When you're pressed for time, make a few quick copies, pass them out, and let the fun and learning begin.

The Love Bug Quiz

Circle one response for each of the following statements. Use the Answer Key at the end to score your quiz.

1. **When I don't have a boyfriend or girlfriend, I feel**

   a. really lonely

   b. OK about myself

   c. like I'm missing out on something

2. **A great date consists of**

   a. plenty of serious, heart-to-heart talk

   b. a movie and a quick drive home

   c. watching television with other friends, lots of laughs

3. **I've been in love**

   a. more times than I can count

   b. never

   c. What's love got to do with it?

4. **When I graduate from high school, I want to**

   a. get married as soon as possible

   b. concentrate on things other than dating

   c. play the field

5. I've learned the most about love from

    a. talking to my friends

    b. talking with my parents

    c. TV/ movies/ music

6. If I had one question about love, it would be

    a. How will I know when it's true love?

    b. How will love change my life?

    c. Will it last?

7. I get tired of people talking about love when

    a. I know they are not sincere

    b. I know they are just bragging

    c. I know how fortunate they are to have someone

8. I'll know someone loves me when

    a. he or she buys me a dozen roses or a nice ring

    b. he or she demonstrates faithfulness and honesty in action

    c. he or she tells me so

Answer Key

The Romantic

If you circled mostly *a* answers, you definitely have a tendency to think of love in terms of flowers, dating, and memories. It will be helpful for you to consider what you truly want in another person. You also tend to need a special person in your life at all times, and when you are not "attached" you feel undervalued. Try waiting for someone who truly loves you, and shows it. Remember: You are worth it.

The Achiever

If you circled mostly *b* answers, you tend to have a level-headed approach to love. You tend to know what you want in another person, and you are willing to wait. You can also concentrate on your own goals, and on what you look for in others in their ability to be compatible with you. You are likely to wait longer before getting married, since you have a patient, methodical outlook on dating and on life.

The Inquisitor

If you circled mostly *c* answers, you are probably looking for love but are unsure how to find it. You tend to have a lot of questions about love and are uncertain of your own feelings sometimes. You are, however, looking for a steady relationship; and you can sometimes get jealous of others who have someone close. Remember how special you are, and never give up on love.

Friendship Follies

Circle one answer for each statement. Use the Answer Key at the end to score your quiz.

1. A best friend is someone who

   a. makes me laugh

   b. is honest and trustworthy

   c. has a nice car

2. I tend to have

   a. just a few close friends

   b. lots of friends

   c. not many friends

3. I feel hurt by a friend when

   a. I am lied to

   b. we have an argument over something petty

   c. I don't get what I want

4. My best friend would most closely resemble

   a. a Hollywood star

   b. the guy or girl next door

   c. a party animal

From LAST-MINUTE MEETINGS, by Todd Outcalt. © 2001 by Abingdon Press.

5. When it comes to friends, my
   motto is

    a. the more the merrier

    b. live and let live

    c. better safe than sorry

6. When I think of the friends I have now,

    a. I feel good about the fun times we've had

    b. I hope we will always be supportive and close

    c. I know I can do better

7. One gift I've been given through friendship is

    a. great memories

    b. the ability to be myself

    c. lots of great stuff

8. Choose one of the following statements:

    a. Who you know is important for success in life.

    b. I'd rather be a friend than have a friend.

    c. A friend in need is no friend of mine.

Answer Key

The Mover and Shaker

If you chose mostly *a* answers, you tend to have a lot of friends; you are the type who really works a room at a party. Friends are important; you often see a friend as someone who can help you succeed or get somewhere in life. Although you have many friends, you may have fewer friends whom you really trust, or who will remain good friends in the years ahead.

The Befriender

If you circled mostly *b* answers, you are someone who values close friends and truthfulness and honesty in all your relationships. You are likely to stick with the same friends through life and will remain close to your closest friends no matter what. You are also more likely to befriend those who need a friend.

The Short-Timer

If you circled mostly *c* answers, you are someone who has fewer friends. You tend to keep to yourself a lot, but you also value having a good time with friends more than the friendships themselves. You are probably looking for a few good friends.

From LAST-MINUTE MEETINGS, by Todd Outcalt. © 2001 by Abingdon Press.

The David Quiz

1. David killed a giant named Goliath. **T** F

2. David was the oldest of seven brothers when he killed Goliath. **T** F

3. David was the second king of Israel. **T** F

4. There was another king who tried to kill David. **T** F

5. David's best friend was Jonathan. **T** F

6. David was a handsome fellow. **T** F

7. King David had an affair with a married woman. **T** F

8. King David had the married woman's husband killed, to cover up his sin. **T** F

9. David was never forgiven for his sin. **T** F

10. All of David's children loved him. **T** F

11. David himself never killed anyone. **T** F

12. God loved David despite his sin. **T** F

13. David built the first Temple in Jerusalem. **T** F

14. David had a son named Solomon. **T** F

15. David was killed in battle and died a hero. **T** F

Answer Key:

1. **T** (1 Samuel 17:50); 2. F (1 Samuel 17:12-14); 3. **T** (1 Samuel 24:20);
4. **T** (1 Samuel 24:2); 5. **T** (1 Samuel 20:17); 6. **T** (1 Samuel 16:12);
7. **T** (2 Samuel 11:3-5); 8. **T** (2 Samuel 11:14-15); 9. F (2 Samuel 12:13);
10. F (2 Samuel 13:30); 11. F (1 Samuel 21:11); 12. **T** (2 Samuel 24:25);
13. F (1 Kings 5:3-5); 14: **T** (1 Kings 1:17); 15: F (1 Kings 2:1-12)

 # Books of the Bible

32

1. The first book of the Bible is Genesis. T F

2. There is a book of the Bible called Hesitations. T F

3. There is a book of the Bible called Lamentations. T F

4. Jesus wrote several books of the Bible. T F

5. Paul wrote most of the books in the New Testament. T F

6. The story of Moses is found in Exodus. T F

7. The story of King David is found in Second Kings. T F

8. The Bible contains no bloodshed, violence, or sex. T F

9. There is a book of the Bible called Galatians. T F

10. There is a book of the Bible called Mutations. T F

11. The last book of the Bible is Revelation. T F

12. There are four Gospels in the New Testament. T F

13. The story of the early church is found in Acts. T F

14. We can read about the life story of James in the Book of James. T F

15. We can read about Ruth in the Book of Ruth. T F

Answer Key:

1. (T); 2 (F); 3 (T); 4 (F); 5 (T); 6 (T); 7 (F); 8 (F); 9 (T); 10 (F); 11 (T); 12 (T); 13 (T); 14 (F); 15 (T)

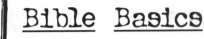 # Bible Basics

Complete the following Bible quotations:

1. In the beginning, God created the _____ and the _____.

2. Moses went to Pharaoh and said _____.

3. Joshua told the people, as for me and my house, we will serve the _____.

4. David put his hand in his bag, took out a _____, slung it, and killed the Philistine.

5. It pleased the Lord that Solomon had asked for _____.

6. For everything there is a _____, and a time for every matter under heaven.

7. Blessed are the _____, for theirs is the kingdom of heaven.

8. An argument arose among the disciples as to which one of them was the _____.

9. Then Jesus, crying out with a loud voice [from the cross] said, "Father, into your hands I commend _____."

10. The women came to the tomb and saw that the _____ had been removed from the tomb.

11. Now as [Saul] was going along and approaching _____, suddenly a light from heaven flashed around him.

12. And now faith, hope, and love abide, and the greatest of these is _____.

Answer Key:

1. heavens/earth (Genesis 1); 2. let my people go (Exodus 7); 3. Lord (Joshua 24);
4. stone (1 Samuel 17); 5. wisdom (2 Chronicles 1); 6. season (Ecclesiastes 3);
7. poor in spirit (Matthew 5); 8. greatest (Mark 9); 9. my spirit (Luke 23);
10. stone (Luke 24); 11. Damascus (Acts 9); 12. love (1 Corinthians 13)

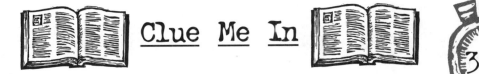

Clue Me In

34

Each clue below is for a book of the Bible. But . . . which book?

1. Ito, Judy, and Amy

2. This book means "second law."

3. Parents don't like to see one or more of these on walls.

4. If this book were a ranch, it might be called THE TRIPLE K.

5. His friends called him Zeke.

6. This book contains the "love chapter."

7. A very "revealing" book

8. If spelled differently, this book could also be used to chop trees.

9. This book is the lead-off hitter in the New Testament.

10. You'd think this book had a lot of math in it.

Answer Key:

1. Judges; 2. Deuteronomy; 3. Mark; 4. Habakkuk; 5. Ezekiel; 6. 1 Corinthians;
7. Revelation; 8. Acts; 9. Matthew; 10. Numbers

From LAST-MINUTE MEETINGS, by Todd Outcalt. © 2001 by Abingdon Press.

Prophets of Old

Choose an answer for each statement about the prophets:

1. Ezekiel was carried into heaven by a fiery chariot. T F

2. The court prophet in David's time was Nathan. T F

3. Jonah never got angry with God. T F

4. Daniel lived during the Babylonian captivity. T F

5. Haggai lived during the Babylonian captivity. T F

6. Hosea took a prostitute as his wife. T F

7. Elisha was the successor to Elijah. T F

8. Zechariah had a vision of a wheel in the sky. T F

9. John the Baptizer was considered a prophet. T F

10. Jeremiah was thrown into a den of lions. T F

Answer Key:

1. F (Elijah); 2. T; 3. F; 4. T; 5. F; 6. T; 7. T; 8. F (Ezekiel); 9. T; 10. F (Daniel)

This Land Is Your Land

36

This quiz will test your knowledge of the lands of the Bible.
Choose an answer for each question:

1. Moses led the Hebrews out of the land of

   a. Goshen   c. Lakes

   b. Egypt   d. Edom

2. The holy mountain where the Israelites received the law was found in

   a. Canaan   c. Moab

   b. Sinai   d. the Rockies

3. During the time of David, the land along the sea belonged to

   a. the Philistines   c. the Gaddites

   b. the parasites   d. the Touchites

4. What river flowed through the heart of Israel and Judah?

   a. the Amazon   c. the Nile

   b. the Big Boy   d. the Jordan

5. When Saul/Paul saw the bright light, he was on his way to

   a. Damascus   c. jail

   b. Jerusalem   d. Wendy's

From LAST-MINUTE MEETINGS, by Todd Outcalt. © 2001 by Abingdon Press.

6. Ezekiel and the captives were taken to what land?

    a. Babylon   c. Syria

    b. Assyria   d. Easter Island

7. The capital of Judah was

    a. Samaria   c. Benjamin

    b. DC   d. Jerusalem

8. Paul claimed to be a citizen of what empire?

    a. Roman   c. Greek

    b. Egyptian   d. Imperial Forces

9. The region where Jesus grew up was called

    a. the playground   c. Galilee

    b. the Decapolis   d. Judea

10. The lowest point on the Earth's surface is

    a. Death Valley   c. the Dead Sea

    b. Dry Gulch   d. Rome

Answer Key:

1. b. (Exodus 19:1); 2. b. (Exodus 19:18); 3. a. (1 Samuel 5:1);
4. d. (Judges 7:24-25); 5. a. (Acts 9:3); 6. a. (2 Kings 25:11);
7. d. (1 Chronicles 11:4-9); 8. a. (Acts 22:25); 9. c. (Luke 2:39); 10. c.

The Disciples

Circle one answer for each statement:

1. Matthew was a

      a. soldier   c. farmer

      b. tax collector   d. mayor

2. James and John were the sons of

      a. Zebedee   c. Earl

      b. Freedom   d. Mary

3. Andrew was the brother of

      a. Martha   c. Simon Peter

      b. Thomas   d. Goliath

4. Peter was a

      a. fisherman   c. doctor

      b. rabbi   d. rich man

5. Peter's original name was

      a. Pinkie   c. Simon

      b. Dude   d. Pete

From LAST-MINUTE MEETINGS, by Todd Outcalt © 2001 by Abingdon Press.

6. What three disciples accompanied Jesus to the top of a mountain?

    a. Andrew, Philip, and James   c. Thomas, Mark, and Luke

    b. Simon, Bartholomew, and Mark   d. Peter, James, and John

7. What disciple had doubts about Jesus' resurrection?

    a. Peter   c. Thomas

    b. James   d. Philip

8. Jesus once sent out how many disciples into the neighboring villages?

    a. 70   c. 40

    b. 12   d. 101

9. The disciple who denied Jesus was named

    a. John   c. James

    b. Peter   d. Luke

10. Which disciple killed himself?

    a. Peter   c. Judas

    b. James   d. Thomas

11. Which disciples were the first to speak of the empty tomb?

    a. the women   c. John and James

    b. Peter and Paul   d. Thomas and Philip

12. Which disciple spoke to the crowd on the day of Pentecost?

    a. Peter   c. John

    b. Paul   d. Thomas

Answer Key:

1. b. (Matthew 9:9); 2. a. (Matthew 4:21); 3. c. (Matthew 4:18) ;
4. a. (Matthew 4:18); 5. c. (Matthew 4:18); 6. d. (Matthew 17:1);
7. c. (John 20:24-28); 8. a. (Luke 10:1); 9. b. (Luke 22:55-57);
10. c. (Matthew 27:3-5); 11. a. (Luke 24:1-10); 12. a. (Acts 2:14)

From LAST-MINUTE MEETINGS, by Todd Outcalt. © 2001 by Abingdon Press.

Proverbs

38

Which of the following proverbs can be found in the Bible? After you take the quiz, discuss what you think each proverb means.

1. A soft answer turns away wrath.

2. Cleanliness is next to godliness.

3. Like a gold ring in a pig's snout is a beautiful woman without good sense.

4. A scoundrel and a villain goes around with crooked speech.

5. A bird in the hand is worth two in the bush.

6. God helps those who help themselves.

7. The fear of the Lord is the beginning of knowledge.

8. From the fruit of their words good persons eat good things.

9. Whoever is slow to anger has great understanding.

10. Those who oppress the poor insult their Maker.

11. The bigger they are, the harder they fall.

12. Grandchildren are the crown of the aged, and the glory of children is their parents.

13. A good name is to be chosen rather than great riches.

14. You can't take it with you.

15. The best things in life are free.

Answer Key:

1. Proverbs 15:1; 2. no; 3. Proverbs 11:22; 4. Proverbs 6:12; 5. no; 6. no;
7. Proverbs 1:7; 8. Proverbs 13:2; 9. Proverbs 14:29; 10. Proverbs 14:31;
11. no; 12. Proverbs 17:6; 13. Proverbs 22:1; 14. no; 15. no

From LAST-MINUTE MEETINGS, by Todd Outcalt. © 2001 by Abingdon Press.

Chapter 5

Sonic Surveys

The surveys in this chapter can help any busy youth leader in a pinch as well as provide useful information. Some of these surveys can be used to determine the desires of the group. Others are simply for enjoyment. Whatever the purpose, each survey is easy to use and can help meet a last-minute need.

Top-Ten Talks

39

Complete this survey, then discuss the results or return the survey to the leader.

10. Spiritually speaking, I'd like to talk about

9. One Bible topic I'd like to talk about is

8. As for relationships I'd like to talk about

7. One subject I'd like to know more about is

6. When it comes to school, I'd like to talk about

5. One thing I don't understand is

4. When it comes to God, I'd like to know

3. One controversial topic that interests me is

2. One thing our group needs to talk about is

1. The most important subject we could talk about is

Name _____ Phone _____ E-mail _____

Top-Ten Places

Complete this survey, then discuss the results or return the survey to your leader.

10. One fun place I'd like to visit is

9. One weekend place I'd like to visit is

8. One beautiful place I'd like to visit is

7. One strange place I'd like to visit is

6. One spiritual place I'd like to visit is

5. One faraway place I'd like to visit is

4. One mission site I'd like to visit is

3. One meaningful place I'd like to visit is

2. One place I'd like to visit every year is

1. The most memorable place for me is

Name _____ Phone _____ E-mail _____

From LAST-MINUTE MEETINGS, by Todd Outcalt. © 2001 by Abingdon Press.

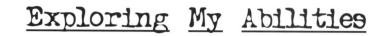

Exploring My Abilities

Complete the survey, then be prepared to discuss what you learned about yourself.

1. The work that excites me the most is

2. Other people say I am gifted at

3. The things I do best involve

4. My greatest enjoyment comes from doing

5. My greatest happiness is derived from

6. I think God has given me the ability to

7. When I work with others to complete a project, I feel

8. When I work alone to accomplish a task, I feel

9. I receive my highest satisfaction from doing

10. If asked to describe my best talent, I would say it is

Name _____ Phone _____ E-mail _____

Theology Shuffle I

Use a 1–4 scale to complete this survey (1 means "I totally disagree" ; 4 means "I totally agree"). Be prepared to discuss your answers.

1. The Bible is always to be understood literally. _ _ _ _ _

2. A Christian is a good person. _ _ _ _ _

3. Racism is always wrong. _ _ _ _ _

4. I have always believed everything I have ever heard about the Christian faith. _ _ _ _ _

5. Gossip is a sin. _ _ _ _ _

6. Christians should agree about everything. _ _ _ _ _

7. The Bible tells us everything we need to know about God. _ _ _ _ _

8. We can encounter God through listening to others. _ _ _ _ _

9. The Bible is a book about good people. _ _ _ _ _

10. Teachers should be allowed to lead students in public prayers. _ _ _

Name _____ Phone _____ E-mail _____

logy Shuffle II

te this survey (1 means "I totally disagree"; 4 means "I
d to discuss your answers.

Identify a Christian by the way he or
one lives. ____

2. National leaders should be held to a higher standard
than others. ____

3. Church leaders should be held to a higher standard
than others. ____

4. Christians should be held to a higher standard than
others. ____

5. The Bible's primary teaching is about God's grace.
____

6. The world is worse than it was a hundred years ago.
____

7. The world will be a better place a hundred years from
now. ____

8. When a person sins, it means God hates that person.
____

9. Pastors and youth leaders are superior spiritual
beings. ____

10. God always answers prayer. ____

Name _____ Phone _____ E-mail_____

From LAST-MINUTE MEETINGS, by Todd Outcalt. © 2001 by Abingdon Press.

I'd Like to . . .

Complete the survey and tally the responses of your group.

44

1. I'd like to have a group session about

2. I'd like to take a trip to

3. I'd like to serve others by

4. I'd like to watch a video about

5. I'd like to sing

6. I'd like to spend a retreat at

7. I'd like to take a mission trip to

8. I'd like to tell others about

9. I'd like to help with

10. I'd like to lead

Name _____ *Phone* _____ *E-mail* _____

Academy Awards

45

Time this survey just prior to the presentation of the Academy Awards. The results for your group could be tallied and posted.

My vote for best picture goes to

My vote for best actor goes to

My vote for best actress goes to

My vote for best supporting actor goes to

My vote for best supporting actress goes to

My vote for best director goes to

My vote for best song in a soundtrack goes to

My vote for best special effects goes to

My vote for best costumes goes to

Name _____ *Phone* _____ *E-mail*_____

Music Awards

This survey is best taken before any of the major music awards shows. The results for your group could be tallied and posted.

My vote for best new artist goes to

My vote for song of the year goes to

My vote for best male recording artist goes to

My vote for best female recording artist goes to

My vote for album of the year goes to

My vote for best soundtrack goes to

My vote for best performer goes to

My vote for best music video goes to

My vote for best musical group goes to

Name _____ Phone _____ E-mail_____

Ministry I'd Like to Do

Complete the following survey. Be prepared to discuss your responses with the group.

1. One need I see in our community is

2. One need I think our group can meet is

3. One talent I have to offer is

4. One need we can pray for each week is

5. I would like to help with

6. I would like to do mission work in

7. One ministry I can do is

Name _____ *Phone* _____ *E-mail* _____

Parent Survey

48

Identify gifts and talents you would be willing to use with the youth group.

1. I am best at helping with

2. The best time for me to help is

3. I am willing to help with or provide the following:

Transportation _____ Meals _____ Snacks _____

Chaperone _____ Prayer _____ Counsel _____

Lead a meeting _____ Weekend/Retreat help _____

Cleanup _____ Setup _____ Communication _____

Other _____

Name _____ *Phone* _____ *E-mail* _____

From LAST-MINUTE MEETINGS, by Todd Outcalt. © 2001 by Abingdon Press.

Songs I Like

Complete the survey and return it to the youth leader.

I'd like to sing the following songs in youth meetings this year:

_____

_____

_____

_____

_____

_____

_____

_____

One song I'd like to talk about is

One song I'd like to sing in worship is

One new song I'd like our group to learn is

My favorite song is

If our group had a theme song, it should be

Name _____ Phone _____ E-mail _____

From LAST-MINUTE MEETINGS, by Todd Outcalt. © 2001 by Abingdon Press.

My Thoughts, Exactly

50

Complete the survey and return it to the youth leader.

1. If I could change one thing about our youth meetings, it would be this:

2. The thing I appreciate most about our group is

3. If I could say one thing to our youth leaders, it would be this:

4. I'm so grateful for

5. I would ask for prayer for

6. The greatest need in my life right now is

7. Here's what I'd like the youth leader to know about me:

8. I would like the youth leader to ___ give me a call or ___ write me.

9. ___ Keep my responses confidential. ___ Pray for my concerns. ___ Provide me with helpful materials.

Name _____ Phone _____ E-mail _____

Chapter 6

Thought-Provoking Puzzles

These tantalizing puzzles will challenge your youth and get their minds working. Word games, riddles, mystery stories, Bible puzzlers, brain-teasers, and more . . . they're all here. Caution: Use these puzzles sparingly to avoid brain burn-out!

Mystery Manor

Instruct the youth to listen carefully as you read aloud the following mystery story. Ham it up and use different voices, if you like. Then give each person a pencil and paper. Ask the questions under "Clues" to see who remembers the most details about this humorous mystery, which is more entertaining than mysterious.

The Story

It was a dark and stormy night when Penelope walked into the old manor on Bat Hill. She had lost an earring and a fingernail while hiking near the grist mill at Creepy Creek. She was relaxing by the fire, when she felt something cold on her shoulder . . . it was a hand! She quickly turned to find that she was not alone.

"Hello," said the stranger. "My name is Warf, and I'll be your host tonight until 3 A.M."

"What is this place," asked Penelope, "and how did I get here?"

"Mystery Manor does strange things to people," Warf mysteriously replied.

Suddenly, a scream came from the kitchen. Penelope and Warf ran to the scene and found a body on the floor. "Look!" Penelope exclaimed. "Someone's taken the #18 carving knife!"

"Yes," said Warf, "and they've used it to slice the lasagna! Have some?"

Penelope and Warf sat down and began eating lasagna. But when they looked up again, the body was gone.

Moments later, the butler appeared with lasagna stains on his chin. "Have you been served?" he asked, carrying the knife in his trembling left hand.

"No thanks," said Penelope. "I've got a long day tomorrow and I need a flashlight."

The butler retired to the parlor; and when Penelope turned around, Warf was gone, too. "Wow," Penelope whispered. "Now we'll never know who did it!"

Do you?

Clues

1. Where was the old manor located? (on Bat Hill)

2. What had Penelope lost? Where? (an earring and a fingernail / grist mill at Creepy Creek)

3. What knife was missing from the kitchen? (the #18 carving knife)

4. What did Penelope and Warf sit down to eat? (lasagna)

5. How long was Warf host at Mystery Manor? (till 3 A.M.)

6. Who do you think did it? (the butler)

Solution to the Mystery

The butler, of course, was not really dead. He had a rare form of palsy and had slipped on the floor and then screamed while cutting the lasagna. When Warf heard that Penelope needed a flashlight, he went to the cellar to find one. He is, after all, a gentleman and only wanted to help her find her lost items.

The Great Bank Robbery

Instruct the youth to listen carefully as you read aloud the following news story. Then give each person (or team) pencils and paper. Ask the questions on the next page to see who remembers the most details about the story.

At precisely 3:47 P.M. on Wednesday, April 23, the Hiawatha National Bank of Grand Roanoke, East Virginia, was robbed at squirt-gun point by three suspects carrying a velvet bag. The first suspect is 5' 9" tall, has dark brown eyes, and pierced ears. His name is Vinnie, and his mother goes by the name of Ethel Crumpet.

The second suspect is 6' 2" short, has green hair, and a blue tattoo on his left arm that says "Surf or Die." Police believe he was accompanied by a girlfriend, Wanda Wanadana, who may have driven the getaway car—a 1991 Yummy with whitewall tires and a "For Sale by Owner" sign taped to the right passenger window.

The third suspect is a guy named Quincy who is 7' 8" tall but goes by the alias "Short Stuff." He likes graham-cracker pie and was last seen on foot near the Riggins Ice Cream and Motor Oil Lunch Stand. Police believe he is armed and legged and is a danger to himself.

Should you have any information about these individuals, please call 555-0154 before midnight tonight, and receive this fabulous set of chop suey knives and a 4-CD collection of Great Country Crooners. All calls are confidential, and will be shared only with the police and fire departments, the mayor, and the TV news media.

Questions

1. Which suspect had the tattoo? What did it say? (The second suspect / Surf or Die)

2. What is the name of the first suspect's mother? (Ethel Crumpet)

3. What bank was robbed? When? (Hiawatha National Bank / 3:47 P.M., April 23)

4. How tall is the third suspect? What is his nickname? (7' 8" / Short Stuff)

5. Where was the third suspect last seen? (the Riggins Ice Cream and Motor Oil Lunch Stand)

6. If you have information, what number should you call? (555-0154)

7. What prizes will you receive if you call before the deadline? When is the deadline? (chop suey knives and 4 CDs / midnight)

8. What is the name of the girlfriend? (Wanda Wanadana)

9. What year and make of car was she driving? (1991 Yummy)

10. What color are the first suspect's eyes? (dark brown)

51

Brain Teasers

See who can identify the following brain teasers. Remember that perspective is everything.

Figure A

Figure B

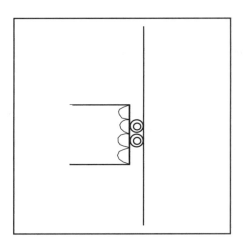

Figure C

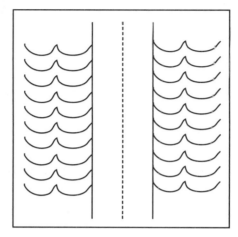

Figure D

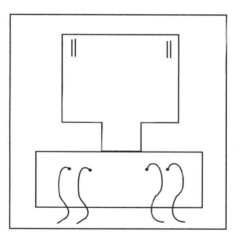

Answer Key:

Figure A: a cowboy frying bacon and eggs (bird's-eye view)

Figure B: an elephant roller-skating up a wall (side view)

Figure C: a bridge over troubled water (bird's-eye view)

Figure D: a computer (rear view)

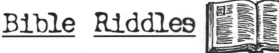

Bible Riddles

Strain your brain to see what Bible character fits each description below:

1. Some might say I lost my head, but I was always in control. **Who am I?**

2. I wasn't ready for a foot-washing, and I fell asleep in the garden. **Who am I?**

3. I've never held up a building, but I'm sure salty right now. **Who am I?**

4. It's not every man who would work 14 years for two wives. **Who am I?**

5. I specialize in talking to Ethiopian eunuchs. **Who am I?**

6. Jawbone of a donkey is no delicacy, but it made a great weapon for me. **Who am I?**

7. Some say I'm a giant-killer. **Who am I?**

8. I was the original survivor when I was shipwrecked on Malta. **Who am I?**

9. The original spin doctor, I spoke for Moses on many occasions. **Who am I?**

10. We weren't the Three Stooges, but we were still wise guys. **Who are we?**

Answer Key:

1. John the Baptizer (Matthew 14:8-11)

2. Peter (John 13:6 and Matthew 26:40)

3. Lot's wife (Genesis 19:26)

4. Jacob (Genesis 29:18, 30)

5. Philip (Acts 8:26-40)

6. Samson (Judges 15:15-16)

7. David (1 Samuel 17:50)

8. Paul (Acts 28:1)

9. Aaron (Exodus 4:14-16)

10. The magi (Matthew 2:1)

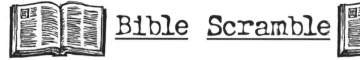

Bible Scramble

53

Unscramble the letters in each item below to form the name of a Bible person:

1. VEE

2. REEPT

3. HAROBED

4. NOJH

5. TTHEWAM

6. RAAHS

7. RCHLAE

8. LUAP

9. KIEEZEL

10. YARM

Answer Key:

1. Eve

2. Peter

3. Deborah

4. John

5. Matthew

6. Sarah

7. Rachel

8. Paul

9. Ezekiel

10. Mary

From LAST-MINUTE MEETINGS, by Todd Outcalt © 2001 by Abingdon Press.

Fun Christmas Puzzler

54

1. What kind of Christmas Eve was it when Santa asked Rudolph to guide his sleigh?

2. What funny song is also known as "Christmas, Don't Be Late"?

3. What character had a corncob pipe and a button nose?

4. Who gives the gifts in the "Twelve Days of Christmas"?

5. What song begins, "O the weather outside is frightful"?

6. In "Jingle Bells," what are we doing all the way?

7. Who are we going to see over the river and through the woods?

8. What is the English title of "O Tannenbaum"?

9. In what song are people dressed in holiday style?

10. What did the little drummer boy give to the Christ child?

Answer Key:

1. Foggy

2. "The Chipmunk Song"

3. Frosty the Snowman

4. My true love

5. "Let It Snow!"

6. Laughing

7. Grandmother

8. "O Christmas Tree"

9. "Silver Bells"

10. A song on his drum

Christmas-Carol Puzzler

What carol contains the phrase, "westward leading, still proceeding"?

What carol contains the phrase, "that glorious song of old"?

3. In what direction does the star lead the three kings?

4. What carol contains the line, "Sing, choirs of angels, sing in exultation"?

5. What song contains the phrase, "shall come to thee, O Israel"?

6. What other title is "O Come, All Ye Faithful" known by?

7. In "Joy to the World," who sings?

8. What carol contains the line, "born is the King of Israel"?

9. Who wrote the words to "Hark! the Herald Angels Sing"?

10. What carol was first sung at midnight mass in Paris, 1847?

Answer Key:

1. "We Three Kings"

2. "It Came Upon the Midnight Clear"

3. Westward

4. "O Come, All Ye Faithful"

5. "O Come, O Come, Emmanuel"

6. "Adeste Fideles"

7. Heaven and nature

8. "The First Noel"

9. Charles Wesley

10. "O Holy Night"

Christmas Cartoons

Try to identify Christmas song titles or common phrases from these 22 cartoons:

From LAST-MINUTE MEETINGS, by Todd Outcalt. © 2001 by Abingdon Press.

Answer Key:

1. "Jingle Bells"

2. "Let It Snow! Let It Snow! Let It Snow!"

3. walking in a winter wonderland

4. "The First Noel" [no L]

5. "Twelve Days of Christmas"

6. "I Saw Three Ships"

7. "O Christmas Tree"

8. "Deck the Halls"

9. "Joy to the World"

10. chestnuts roasting on an open fire

11. "It Came Upon a Midnight Clear"

12. "All I Want for Christmas Is My Two Front Teeth"

13. "Here Comes Santa Claus"

14. "O Little Town of Bethlehem"

15. "O Holy Night"

16. "Rudolph the Rednosed Reindeer"

17. "We Three Kings"

18. I'm dreaming of a white Christmas

19. "What Child Is This?"

20. "Away in a Manger"

21. "Silent Night"

22. "I Saw Mommy Kissing Santa Claus"

From LAST-MINUTE MEETINGS, by Todd Outcalt. © 2001 by Abingdon Press.

Paul's Travels

57

Across	Down
1. Scripture scholar and minister to church at Corinth	1. Beginning point of Paul's mission
2. Unclean animals	2. Led Ethiopian eunuch to conversion and baptism
3. Whippersnapper	12. First travel companion of Paul
4. Bull	14. Location of troubled church
5. Greek verb tense	24. Abbreviation: Underwriter's Lab
6. Asia Minor church	25. Pearly clam
7. Feared beast	26. Adjective: true
8. Abbreviation: Optical	27. Deoxyribonucleic acid
9. Ratio of circumference	28. Abbreviation: South Carolina
10. Caesar's home	29. Russian grain
11. Was Saul	30. United States
12. Inexpensive pen	31. Creator
13. Paul spoke of seven	32. Abbreviation: *Sports Illustrated*
14. Greek Messiah	33. Function word of movement
15. First Christian martyr	34. Goal
16. All lead to Rome	35. Nothing
17. Greek god of wine	36. Greek Island
18. Possessive: King of Bashan	37. Night bird
19. Collection of sayings	38. One of seven churches in Revelation
20. Wrongdoings	39. Philippi lies in this colony.
21. Hello	40. Abbreviation: Tennessee
22. Language of OT	41. A stop on Paul's missionary journeys
23. Function word of location	42. State of humanity
	43. Tribe of Israel
	44. Fish hide
	45. Sixty minutes
	46. New Testament

From LAST-MINUTE MEETINGS, by Todd Outcalt. © 2001 by Abingdon Press.

Answer Key:

A¹	P	O	L	L	O²⁵	S²⁶	■	D²⁷	■	P²	I	G	S²⁸
N	■	■	■	Y³	O	U	N	G³¹	■	H	■	■	C
T⁴	A²⁴	R²⁹	U³⁰	S	■	A⁵	O	R	I	S³²	T³³	■	■
I	L⁶	Y	S	T	R	A³⁴	D	■	L⁷	I	O	N³⁵	
O⁸	P	E	E	■	I	■	■	P⁹	I	■	■	I	
C	■	■	■	R¹⁰	O³⁷	M	E³⁸	■	P¹¹	A	U	L	
H	B¹²	I	C³⁶	■	W	■	P	M³⁹	■	■	■		
■	A	■	O	■	L	H¹³	E	A	V	E⁴¹	N	S⁴²	
C¹⁴	H	R	I	S	T⁴⁰	E	■	C	■	P	■	I	
O	N	■	N	■	■	S¹⁵	T	E	P	H	E	N	
R¹⁶	O	A	D⁴³	S⁴⁴	■	U	■	D	■	E	■	N	
I	B¹⁷	A	C	C	H⁴⁵	U	S	■	O¹⁸	G	S	E	
N	A¹⁹	N	A	■	O	■	■	N	■	U	■	R	
T	■	S	■	L	U	■	S²⁰	I	N⁴⁶	S	■	S	
H²¹	I	■	H²²	E	B	R	E	W	■	A²³	T	■	

Revelation Word Puzzle

58

```
G  L  Y  O  D  F  C  Y  R  S  T  A  L  V  R
C  T  R  U  M  P  E  T  S  C  M  S  D  K  O
H  H  H  E  A  V  E  N  R  R  N  L  A  M  B
U  O  O  R  P  N  A  T  I  O  N  S  X  E  A
R  U  R  Y  O  V  G  H  D  L  V  Y  W  Q  B
C  S  N  K  V  N  O  E  W  L  E  L  M  D  Y
H  A  S  U  W  L  E  T  L  O  T  Q  Y  Q  L
E  N  P  J  E  R  U  S  A  L  E  M  U  W  O
S  D  I  O  U  H  V  W  S  T  D  Q  A  S  N
N  A  R  H  S  D  E  F  G  T  W  E  L  V  E
E  T  I  N  M  T  G  P  D  A  H  W  A  A  U
V  A  T  N  T  Q  L  M  U  M  O  O  W  D  G
E  M  R  N  T  K  Z  E  E  B  O  O  K  S  A
S  E  N  T  Z  S  W  D  S  N  T  X  R  G  L
U  N  L  E  H  Z  J  T  M  I  T  S  Y  G  P
```

AMEN	DEAD	PLAGUE
ANGEL	EARTH	SAINTS
APOSTLES	HEAVEN	SCROLL
BABYLON	HORNS	SEVEN
BEAST	JERUSALEM	SPIRIT
BOOKS	JOHN	THOUSAND
BOWLS	JUDGMENT	THRONE
CHURCHES	LAMB	TRUMPETS
CRYSTAL	NATIONS	TWELVE

Answer Key:

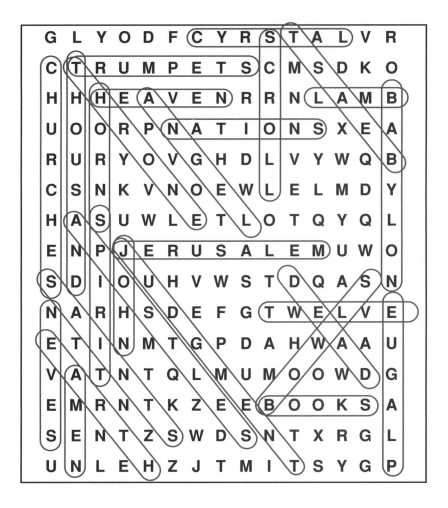

Psalms Word Puzzle

59

```
K R L D L P K C H I T P Y S S
V E V E R L A S T I N G E C M
N J G L A D N E S S I M R O S
S O L I O H Z S V T S I C M G
H I O V Q R Z V H R I E P P F
E C R E R N N X J D C H K A U
P E I R R P E T Q P S O W S D
H M F A I T H F U L N E S S Z
E O Y N S X Y S W H G Z D I F
R S W C S T R E N G T H S O R
D E I E H P W Q P F O N R N J
W W F A U M B P J O Q G N V Q
Z A N U R C Q E Y T I D M V U
H K I W G P L J I V I B B E L
S U N S D E S S E L B B N E M
```

AWESOME	GLORIFY
BLESSED	PRAISE
COMPASSION	REFUGE
DELIVERANCE	REJOICE
EVERLASTING	SHEPHERD
FAITHFULNESS	STRENGTH
FORGIVE	THANKS
GLADNESS	

From LAST-MINUTE MEETINGS, by Todd Outcalt. © 2001 by Abingdon Press.

Answer Key:

```
K  R  L  D  L  P  K  C  H  I  T  P  Y  S  S
V  E  V  E  R  L  A  S  T  I  N  G  E  C  M
N  J  G  L  A  D  N  E  S  S  I  M  R  O  S
S  O  L  I  O  H  Z  S  V  T  S  I  C  M  G
H  I  O  V  Q  R  Z  V  H  R  I  E  P  P  F
E  C  R  E  R  N  N  X  J  D  C  H  K  A  U
P  E  I  R  R  P  E  T  Q  P  S  O  W  S  D
H  M  F  A  I  T  H  F  U  L  N  E  S  S  Z
E  O  Y  N  S  X  Y  S  W  H  G  Z  D  I  F
R  S  W  C  S  T  R  E  N  G  T  H  S  O  R
D  E  I  E  H  P  W  Q  P  F  O  N  R  N  J
W  W  F  A  U  M  B  P  J  O  Q  G  N  V  Q
Z  A  N  U  R  C  Q  E  Y  T  I  D  M  V  U
H  K  I  W  G  P  L  J  I  V  I  B  B  E  L
S  U  N  S  D  E  S  S  E  L  B  B  N  E  M
```

Jonah Word Puzzle

60

```
S  A  C  R  I  F  I  C  E  C  F  T  X  W  B
A  S  T  A  K  D  C  A  P  T  A  I  N  U  E
I  H  R  E  P  E  N  T  M  R  O  T  S  C  L
L  E  B  S  U  N  I  N  E  V  E  H  H  H  L
O  S  W  A  L  L  O  W  B  E  E  F  I  E  Y
R  A  I  R  R  S  O  R  Y  B  C  B  P  S  C
S  C  N  S  O  A  N  G  R  Y  W  Q  X  I  R
Y  K  D  E  L  I  V  E  R  A  N  C  E  P  E
A  C  L  E  T  F  W  K  A  X  R  J  F  U  M
R  L  C  O  E  R  A  N  I  M  A  L  S  N  F
P  O  A  L  E  P  V  J  P  N  I  E  F  Y  L
Y  T  R  O  F  H  E  E  B  I  G  T  Y  Y  W
H  H  G  T  A  R  S  H  I  S  H  U  T  J  X
O  X  O  S  W  O  V  N  J  X  Y  D  O  A  Q
H  B  L  C  W  B  L  N  U  T  B  L  S  B  I
```

AMITTAI	FORTY	SEA
ANGRY	HEBREW	SHEOL
ANIMALS	KING	SHIP
ASHES	LOTS	STORM
BELLY	MERCY	SUN
BUSH	NINEVEH	SWALLOW
CAPTAIN	PRAY	TARSHISH
CARGO	REPENT	VOWS
DEEP	SACKCLOTH	WAVES
DELIVERANCE	SACRIFICE	WIND
FISH	SAILORS	

Answer Key:

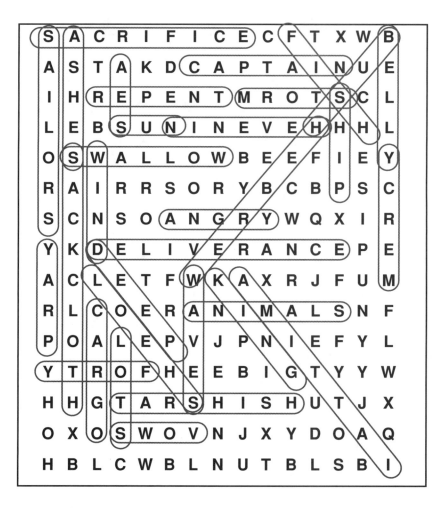

John & Jesus Word Puzzle

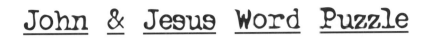

61

```
M M F K G E Y D G A L I L E E
A Q Q U D E X X B P W B U M W
R Z B A P T I Z E D G R O O D
Y E E N P D J F I N X L M O B
E C H D V N E L I Z A B E T H
N H E R O D G Z L S P I R I T
O A A E U L L E T P E L O N M
H R D W I L D E R N E S S C B
E I E R P U N T J B M Z N R J
A A D L O R C J B E L O V E D
V H V P W J U D E A K L U A G
E R E H T A E L O C U S T S U
N A Z A R E T H E V Z X J E A
S L A D N A S E H Y E U H A K
V J J T S D E C R E A S E D A
```

ANDREW	HEROD	NAZARETH
BAPTIZED	HONEY	SALOME
BEHEADED	INCREASE	SANDALS
BELOVED	JORDAN	SPIRIT
DECREASE	JUDEA	WATER
DOVE	LEATHER	WILDERNESS
ELIZABETH	LOCUSTS	WOMB
GALILEE	MARY	ZECHARIAH
HEAVENS		

From LAST-MINUTE MEETINGS, by Todd Outcalt. © 2001 by Abingdon Press.

Answer Key:

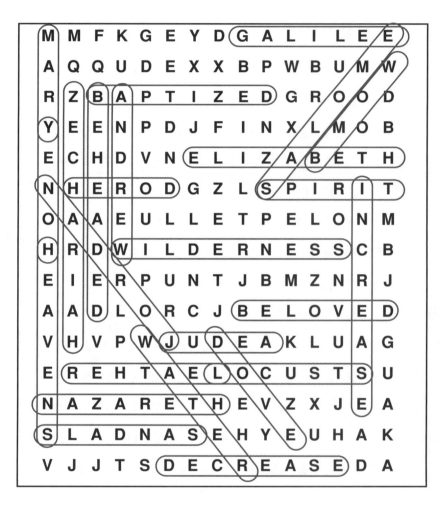

Chapter 7

Tantalizing Talks

Here are 15 fine-tuned talks that you can use to open or close a meeting, or as a devotional tool. You're sure to find a theme or topic broad enough to speak to your group or situation. Use the reflection questions as guides to lengthen the talk, or as a time for talkback with the youth. As always, feel free to adapt these talks to fit the specific needs of your youth.

Pleasing God

Theme: Integrity

Scripture: Psalm 19:14 ("Let the words of my mouth and the meditation of my heart be acceptable to you, O LORD, my rock and my redeemer.")

The Greek teacher Aesop once told a tale about a father and a son who were bringing a donkey to market. *(The following text is an adaptation of the story.)* As they passed along the road, they heard someone say, "Look at those silly people—walking beside a donkey when they could be riding him!"

When the father heard this, he and his son sat on the donkey's back and continued on their way. Farther up the road, another person commented, "Look at that pair—both of them riding on the back of that poor donkey!"

So the father got off and let his son ride. But someone else commented, "Look at that disrespectful boy—riding a donkey and making his poor father walk!"

When the son heard this, he got off and let his father ride. Another person said, "Look at that horrible father—riding on the donkey and making his son walk!"

The father and son eventually hit upon another idea. They started carrying the donkey, thinking no one would complain about that. But as they struggled on, they eventually lost control of the heavy animal and it fell into the river and drowned.

The moral of the fable is, Those who try to please everyone end up pleasing no one.

Ultimately, our goal in life is to please God. When we chart our course by others' standards, we are not being true to ourselves or to God. But when we make decisions based on what is pleasing and acceptable to God, not on what is popular, we show integrity and faithfulness unto God. Today's Scripture lesson is perhaps the best definition of integrity. Praying always that our words and meditations are pleasing and acceptable to God is a sure way to worship God in all we say and do. By living a life of worship we live a life of integrity and faithfulness.

For Reflection:

In what ways might trying to please others backfire?

Why might it be harder for us to focus on pleasing God, than on pleasing others?

What insights do you gain from the Scripture passage?

Road Rage

Theme: Helpfulness

Scripture: 1 Corinthians 12:28 ("And God has appointed in the church first apostles, second prophets, third teachers; then deeds of power, then gifts of healing, forms of assistance, forms of leadership, various kinds of tongues.")

Who are you? That question may seem strange; but when we consider the Scripture lesson, we realize that God gives everyone different gifts and talents. We may not live out our discipleship the same way, but we can all be in service to God. Reflect on this story about a man who went out of his way to share his gift with others:

When you hear the words *road rage,* you may think of someone getting very angry while driving on a busy highway. However, rage can also be defined as enthusiasm. Here is an example: Out on the roads of southern California a guy named Tom Weller is practicing a different brand of passion. For over thirty years now, he's been driving the interstate highways in his 1955 Ford, looking for people in trouble.

Perhaps it's someone with a dry radiator, or maybe someone who has run out of gas. Tom Weller has helped thousands of people change flat tires, jumpstart their car, or even find the nearest service station. He's out on the highway to assist those who are in need, and we can only hope that his form of road rage catches on.

Tom Weller is enthusiastic about helping people along the road. He never expects money in return. He does it because helping others makes him feel good. He does it because helping people is his gift. He hopes that those he helps will continue the cycle of helping others in need.

Being a helpful person is only one of the gifts of the spirit. Others are preaching, teaching, prophesying, healing, leading, and speaking. God gave each one different gifts so that we, the church, could build one another up and reach more people with the gospel. Though some people may have different gifts, we can all do something to serve others. So the next time you think being helpful doesn't matter, think about Tom Weller and consider all the people he has helped. Remember his good advice: If someone shows you an act of kindness, pass it along as quickly as possible.

For Reflection:

♡ What gift do you think you have?

How do you enjoy helping others?

What could you do to use your gift this week?

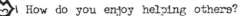

Choices

Theme: Making Decisions

Scripture: Psalm 32:8 ("I will instruct you and teach you the way you should go; I will counsel you with my eye upon you.")

The teenage years are filled with choices and important decisions. Whether it's a decision about dating, homework, or even college, God is there to guide you.

The world-famous tenor Luciano Pavarotti struggled before choosing his ultimate career. When he was a boy, his father encouraged Pavarotti to take voice lessons. Later, when Pavarotti was enrolled in a teaching institute, he was a pupil of Arrigo Pola, a famous voice teacher in his hometown. Pavarotti came to love both teaching and the singing of music. He was torn between the two disciplines. One day Pavarotti asked his father: What should I do? Be a teacher or a singer?

His father replied, Always remember this. If you try to sit in two chairs, you will fall between them. For life, you must choose only one chair.

Some decisions are bigger or more important than others, but we do not have to face any of them alone. The Scripture lesson assures us that God watches over us and offers us wisdom for the tough choices we often have to make. Do not neglect God's help in making decisions. God promises to instruct us and keep an eye on us. God guides us so that we will never "fall between the chairs."

For Reflection:

What difficult choices have you faced in your life?

How did God help you face those choices?

What are some ways to seek God's instruction in decision-making?

114

What's That?

Theme: Communication

Scripture: Proverbs 2:1-2 ("My child, if you accept my words and treasure up my commandments within you, making your ear attentive to wisdom and inclining your heart to understanding; if you indeed cry out for insight, and raise your voice for understanding; if you seek it like silver, and search for it as for hidden treasures— then you will understand the fear of the LORD and find the knowledge of God.")

"Accept my words," "[make] your ear attentive," "[incline] your heart to understanding," "cry out for insight," "seek [understanding] like silver, and search for it as for hidden treasures"—all of these are examples of what it means to truly communicate, with God and with others. Do we communicate only by talking and hearing, or do we also listen attentively and search for understanding and insight?

Radio host Paul Harvey told a humorous story some years ago about a fellow who went to the doctor with an ache in his right ear. The doctor performed a simple examination and then prescribed an antibiotic. "Take this to the pharmacy, use it as indicated, and you should have relief from the earache in a matter of hours."

The patient took the prescription to the pharmacy and had it filled. The pharmacist, wanting to save time, wrote: "Apply one drop to R ear." The patient thought the instructions read, "Apply one drop to Rear." "I thought it was a strange way to treat an ear infection," the patient later told his doctor, "but I just followed the directions!"

How often have we been misinformed or misunderstood something that someone was trying to tell us? How often have we miscommunicated with someone else?

Hearing, listening, receiving, and responding are all needed for effective communication. What we say, how we say it, and how we show it are also powerful communication tools. Today's Scripture lesson teaches us that when others talk to us, we should listen not only with our ears, but also with our heart.

For Reflection:

✉ When or how have you experienced miscommunication?

⚔ What could have prevented or corrected the problem?

👄 What, besides speaking, also communicates how we think and feel?

✏ How can God help us communicate with one another more effectively?

👤 How do you think God most commonly communicates with us today?

Gratitude

Theme: Prayer

Scripture: Matthew 6:6 ("But whenever you pray, go into your room and shut the door and pray to your Father who is in secret; and your Father who sees in secret will reward you.")

The legend of King Alfonso XII of Spain says he observed that some of his court attendants neglected to pray before eating, and so he devised a way to teach them a lesson. He had a banquet prepared; invited guests; and watched as each person entered, ate, and left without giving thanks to God. Secretly the king had arranged for a beggar to wander into the hall, seat himself at the head table, and begin eating as everyone was looking on. The other guests were appalled. When the beggar finished his meal, he got up from the table and left the banquet hall. Someone near the king said, "What an ungrateful fellow. He didn't even say thank you!"

The king rose and said, "Do you not realize that all of you have been ungrateful as well? Every day you sit down to a table abundantly provided by your heavenly Father, yet you neither ask his blessing nor express your gratitude."

How about you and me? Have we adequately expressed our thanks to God today? Have we taken for granted the abundant blessings of God? How many times have we gone about the business of our lives and forgotten to include God?

In our Scripture lesson, Jesus says that God does not expect us to always walk around praying loudly and trying to look "godly." On the contrary, Jesus tells us that prayer is a private matter—intimate in nature, as with two good friends who can sit down together and discuss life. We are important to God. God loves it when we take time to pray and spend time with God. Every day we have the opportunity, no matter where we are or what we are doing, to give thanks and to ask God for help and guidance. Let us remember to pray when we're thankful, when we're worried, when we're awed, and every other time we just need to be with God.

For Reflection:

What are you most thankful for today?

What keeps us from being thankful people?

Why, do you think, did Jesus emphasize private prayer over public prayer?

What does Jesus teach us about prayer?

Trash Talk

Theme: Forgiveness

Scripture: Matthew 6:12-15 ("And forgive us our debts, as we also have forgiven our debtors. . . . For if you forgive others their trespasses, your heavenly Father will also forgive you; but if you do not forgive others, neither will your Father forgive your trespasses.")

(**Note:** "And forgive us our trespasses, as we forgive those who trespass against us," an alternate wording for verse 12 based on verse 15, appears in some church rituals and in some versions of the Lord's Prayer set to music.)

A little boy was praying beside his mother in church when the pastor began to lead the congregation in the Lord's Prayer. The mother listened as her son tried to echo the words of the prayer, and tried to hold in laughter when she heard the boy say, "Forgive us our trash baskets, as we forgive those who put trash in our baskets."

These may not be the words Jesus intended, but they have a similar meaning. People sometimes make things difficult for us, just as we sometimes make life difficult for others. We all have to deal with "trash talk" or other forms of abuse on occasion. Likewise, we sometimes put this kind of trash into the lives of others.

Forgiving someone who has hurt or harmed us in some way is most difficult; but it can be done with God's help. The next time you pray (or sing) the Lord's Prayer and say the words, "Forgive us our trespasses, as we forgive those who trespass against us," examine the ways in which you hurt others, whether by word or by deed. Ask God to forgive you for each individual incident. In the same way, ask God to help you forgive those who have hurt you, hurt by hurt. By acknowledging to God each time you've been hurt and each time you've hurt someone else, you are also admitting to yourself that these incidents were in fact hurtful. When we recognize our hurts, they are much easier to forgive and joy is much more abundant.

For Reflection:

 Whom do you need to forgive today?

From whom do you need forgiveness? For what?

High Jump

Theme: Perseverance

Scripture: Philippians 3:13-14 ("Beloved, I do not consider that I have made it my own; but this one thing I do: forgetting what lies behind and straining forward to what lies ahead, I press on toward the goal for the prize of the heavenly call of God in Christ Jesus.")

How high do you think you can jump? I'm sure we have all seen the Olympic high-jump event. The athletes who compete in this event have worked hard at mastering their sport. They continue to set the bar ever higher and train every day to achieve new heights. When high-jumpers fail to reach their mark, they get up and try again until they do, and then they raise the bar even higher. They have to persevere through their defeats and failures so that they can grow as athletes.

In life we also set goals for ourselves. Perhaps we set standards for behavior, school performance, or musical or athletic performance. Maybe we even set targets for ourselves financially, socially, or personally. Reaching these goals can be another matter. Some people may set their goals so low that they easily reach their mark. Others may set their sights very high, but often fail to achieve them.

In our Scripture lesson, Paul gives us a new way to think about reaching our goals. He tells us, Forget the past. Do not dwell on your failures. Press on toward the ultimate goal, which is being like Christ. This is the call of God for each of us.

Keeping our eyes fixed on Jesus will help us meet the standards we set for all other areas of our lives. When being like Christ is the ultimate achievement, every other decision helps us reach that goal. When we take our eyes off that vision, we are more prone to failure. That is not to say our lives will always be perfect if our eyes are fixed on Jesus. Experiencing failure is part of what it means to be human. Living our lives fixed on being like Jesus Christ means that every decision we make leads us either closer to or further away from that goal.

Like the high-jumper, we must always be looking to set the bar higher until every goal or standard we set for ourselves leads us another step closer to Christlikeness. When we fail, we can be sure that God's grace and peace will help us get up, forget about it, and press on again.

For Reflection:

 Which is better: to set low standards and reach them, or to set high standards and sometimes fail? Which do you think you do most often?

What does it mean to become like Christ, a seemingly unattainable goal?

For Goodness' Sake

Theme: Grace

Scripture: Romans 8:31 ("What then are we to say about these things? If God is for us, who is against us?")

Rosalee Coaxum, in South Carolina, has carried on a family tradition all her life. She makes baskets out of bulrushes, a grass that grows along the banks of the river. Rosalee collects the grass herself, then gently weaves it into a work of art. Her mother and grandmother both made the baskets, as well as her great-great-grandmother who was brought to America on a slave ship in the eighteenth century.

Rosalee sees the heritage of basket-weaving as a work of grace. Her great-great-grandfather wove baskets out of bulrushes in Africa. Now she weaves the same baskets in gratitude for the gifts of freedom, love, and family. She makes baskets to continue the tradition and to remember the trials her family has overcome.

How often have we given up on a problem or a difficulty or let go of the past in order to free ourselves from unpleasant memories? Rosalee feels that every task can be a work of healing, one piece of grass at a time. Making baskets reminds her of how far God has brought her and how much God has given to her and her family.

She remembers that, long ago, God delivered the infant Moses from a basket floating in the bulrushes. Though enslaved, Moses later became the leader of a great nation. Because God is always for us, we can always overcome any obstacles.

God helps us in all our defeats, challenges, sorrows, and pain. God can help us overcome so that we can see the beauty of God's grace even in life's difficulties. Don't ever give up or give in to despair. When life gives you lemons, make lemonade. Or when life gives you nothing but weeds, weave a basket of love.

We may often feel separated from God's love. But even when we feel alienated from God, we can be certain that God is near to us. Nothing can separate us from God's love.

For Reflection:

What makes this Scripture passage an especially powerful promise?

How have you experienced God's grace in your life?

How have you experienced God's grace in difficult times?

How might our difficulties be opportunities for God's strength and grace to shine?

Enthusiasm

Theme: Enthusiasm

Scripture: Philippians 4:4 ("Rejoice in the Lord always; again I will say, Rejoice.")

Few things make us feel as used up as being unenthusiastic about a task. Likewise, when we feel used up it's hard to be enthusiastic about any task. We feel exhausted when we are asked to participate in something that seems spiritually dead, useless, or hopeless.

On the other hand, we feel charged up and eager to go when we are involved in something that involves our gifts and our talents, where our efforts make a difference to others.

Perhaps you have been swept up in enthusiasm recently—maybe with the success of your sports team, because you were asked to participate in something you enjoy, or because you felt a spirit of unity and togetherness. Maybe you achieved something special and you wanted to tell others about it.

Wouldn't it be nice to have this same feeling of enthusiasm every day—at school, at home, about our education, or even our youth group? With the benefit of enthusiasm, there would be no end to what we could accomplish together.

The apostle Paul urges us to rejoice always—to have an excitement and an enthusiasm about our faith. Sometimes rejoicing is difficult; but when we remember that God is the source of all good things, the source of our strength and comfort, we can rejoice because God is good, even in the hard times.

For Reflection:

 What makes you enthusiastic?

What are you excited about today?

Why is it sometimes difficult to rejoice?

What excites you the most about God?

Worrywarts

Theme: Worry

Scripture: Matthew 6:25, 33 ("Therefore I tell you, do not worry about your life.... But strive first for the kingdom of God and [God's] righteousness, and all these things will be given to you as well.")

Most human beings are guilty of being worrywarts. When we are young, we worry about little things. As we get older, we begin to worry about being accepted and being popular. In early adulthood, we worry about job security, relationships, or education. Later on, we worry about finances and children. Much later, we worry about security and health issues.

In this Scripture passage, Jesus basically tells us that worrying is a waste of time. Jesus says that, instead of worrying, we are to "strive first for the kingdom of God and [God's] righteousness." Worrying keeps our focus on us. If we are striving first for the kingdom of God, then we are focused on loving God and neighbor. Our lives are lived as an outward expression of God's love within us. If we put all the energy we waste worrying into an eagerness for prayer and righteousness, then our worries will fade because we'll be too busy living God's love.

While we are striving for the Kingdom, God promises to meet our needs. We may not always agree with God about what those needs are, but we can be sure that God knows each and every one. What does Jesus say about the birds, or the lilies of the field? He says that God cares for them even though they don't do anything. How much more does God care for us, God's children? Why should we worry about our lives? God's love is sufficient to care for our needs today, tomorrow, and forever.

Toward that end, you might ask yourself: What worries keep me from having faith in God's tomorrow? Jesus tells us that tomorrow has enough worries of its own. The beauty of tomorrow is that God is there ready and waiting to meet our needs. "Strive first for the kingdom of God and [God's] righteousness." Live with the hope and joy that comes not from worrying, but from seeking God in everything you do. God will heal your worrywarts!

For Reflection:

Why, do you think, do we worry?

What does the Scripture passage say to you about your worries?

How will you overcome your tendency to worry?

Be Patient

Theme: Patience

Scripture: Galatians 5:22-23a ("By contrast, the fruit of the Spirit is love, joy, peace, patience, kindness, generosity, faithfulness, gentleness, and self-control.")

A classic line about patience goes like this: "Lord, give me patience . . . and I want it right now!" How true is that statement for you?

When we know our purpose, patience comes much more easily. For example, if we know today what we need to do tomorrow, we are more likely to have a plan. Thus we feel less rushed and more patient as we go about the day. Without a plan, we can feel hurried, rushed, or out of control.

Life would be easier if we had a plan to define and accomplish all our tasks. Once we know our goal, we also realize that all worthy pursuits take time, energy, and effort. No worthy goal can be achieved with just a small amount of effort or a small investment of time. Patience is one of the most important requirements.

Take learning to play a musical instrument or a sport. These endeavors take practice, practice, and more practice. Shortcuts seldom lead to a desired end. Time is essential in mastering a sport or an instrument. Patience comes easily when we realize this fact, stretch ourselves, and then leave the rest to God.

Today's Scripture lesson teaches us that in order to live by the Spirit, we must also bear the fruit of the Spirit (love, joy, peace, *patience*, kindness, generosity, faithfulness, gentleness, and self-control). Patience allows us to fully experience and live out the other gifts. When we are patient, it is easier to love, be kind, give, and be in control. Patience gives us the needed perspective to allow ourselves to be God's.

What are you trying to achieve? How much time should you realistically give yourself to achieve these goals? Once you can answer these questions, you might become a much more patient person. Are you patient enough to allow yourself to love? Are you patient enough to be in control? Ask God to reveal the fruits of the Spirit within you. Patiently seek God's help in accomplishing your goals.

For Reflection:

Which fruits of the Spirit do you possess? Which are you working on?

In what ways do you need to be a more patient person?

In what ways in your life have you received patience from others? from God?

Fear Not!

Theme: Overcoming Fear

Scripture: 2 Timothy 1:7 ("For God did not give us a spirit of cowardice, but rather a spirit of power and of love and of self-discipline.")

Of all the plagues of humanity, fear is one of the most crippling. Fear keeps us burdened by the past and despairing of the future. Fear locks us into the mindset that we are not good enough or strong enough to make it on our own. The truth is that we aren't. But in Christ, God gives us a spirit of power, love, and self-discipline that enables us to overcome our fears.

Martin Luther, a sixteenth-century church reformer, was feeling fearful and uncertain as to whether there was any hope in life. One day his wife showed up at the breakfast table wearing a black armband. When Luther asked who died, his wife replied that from the way he had been acting, she thought God was dead.

Sometimes we live as if God were dead. Sometimes we go through life with a gloomy outlook, or with an attitude that things can never get better. Sometimes it's easier to settle into our fears than to step out on faith and let go of them.

We need to be reminded that, even in the worst of life's situations or just during uncomfortable moments, God will grant us the strength and power to meet any challenge or test. We are never out of the realm of God's love. Have certain fears invaded your life? Turn them over to God in the spirit of love and power.

For Reflection:

What are your greatest fears in life?

How can fear cripple our motivation and our energy?

What usually happens when we put aside our fears and take a chance?

In what ways or situations might fear be a good thing?

Windows to the Soul

Theme: Jealousy

Scripture: Proverbs 16:18 ("Pride goes before destruction, and a haughty spirit before a fall.")

Back in the late 1800's there were two famous artists who worked with stained glass. One was John La Farge (now relatively unknown) and the other was Louis Comfort Tiffany (you may have heard of Tiffany's in New York or the famous Tiffany glass). At one time, these men were the best of friends. La Farge admired Tiffany's work, and Tiffany returned the admiration.

In 1880, La Farge invented a revolutionary new process for producing stained glass. He showed his new creation to Tiffany, who began using it immediately, producing some of the most magnificent works of art. La Farge had invented the process, but Tiffany seemed to be getting the most recognition. This caused a rift between the two men, which eventually resulted in a bitter lawsuit and a lifelong hatred.

If you visit the Trinity Episcopal Church in Buffalo, New York, you will find examples of La Farge's work and of Tiffany's—huge walls of stained-glass windows that sit side-by-side, each produced by the men who hated each other. Other examples appear separately in other churches, where people gaze upon these images during their worship of God. How ironic that these artists' largest works are found inside places that stand for God's love and peace in the world.

Jealousy can easily lead to hatred. But as the wise words of Proverbs remind us, a proud spirit leads to a fall. If you have had a falling out with someone, give peace a chance. Peace is far more beautiful than jealousy.

For Reflection:

How might the two men have gotten past their initial jealousy and moved ahead as friends or partners?

What would each of them have had to do or change?

What types of pride do you see most prominently displayed today?

How might jealousy ruin a relationship?

How might God help us overcome pride and find peace with others?

Tongue-Twisters

Theme: Truthfulness

Scripture: Ephesians 4:15 ("But speaking the truth in love, we must grow up in every way into him who is the head, into Christ.")

We have all heard certain tongue-twisters like, "She sells seashells by the seashore" or "Peter Piper picked a peck of pickled peppers." Another one is, "Robert gave Richard a rap in the rib for roasting the rabbit so rare." And, if you've not yet heard it, try repeating this tongue-twister, which many people consider the most difficult in the world: "The sixth sick sheik's sixth sheep's sick."

Tongue-twisters are difficult to say—that's what makes them tongue-twisters. But consider how difficult it is for us to say other kinds of words, too. For example, it may be daringly difficult for us to say, "I'm sorry," when we've wronged someone. Or we might find it a bit awkward to say, "I need help." Or maybe we've gotten tongue-tied just trying to say, "I love you."

Sometimes the truth is the most difficult tongue-twister of all. Remember how hard it was to hide the truth from a parent when you were small? Or how difficult it was to say anything coherent when you were caught in a lie for the first time? Being able to admit our shortcomings and failures to others, to ask for help, or being able to say exactly what we mean, are all great signs of maturity, even though such conversations may sometimes be unpleasant.

Don't let your tongue tie up your feelings, your faith, or your future. Always speak the truth in love.

For Reflection:

 What are some situations when speaking the truth in love is difficult?

When have you felt you had to resort to a "little white lie"? or to saying nothing?

Why is speaking the truth in love often difficult?

Can speaking the truth in love be painful? How?

Why are love and truth intertwined?

Wonder

Theme: Awe of God

Scripture: Psalm 19:1-4 ("The heavens are telling the glory of God; and the firmament proclaims [God's] handiwork. Day to day pours forth speech, and night to night declares knowledge. There is no speech, nor are there words; their voice is not heard; yet their voice goes out through all the earth, and their words to the end of the world.")

Perhaps you've heard the phrase, Wonder is a word to wonder about. In fact, there are many awesome moments in life—times and places and events when we know that God is real, or when we sense the awesome wonder of God's love.

Have you ever felt insignificant looking up at the stars at night? or seen a rainbow in the clouds? or stood on the shore of the ocean and looked out over the vastness of the sea? or looked down into the splendor of the Grand Canyon?

If you've had times and moments like these, chances are you've also experienced some sense of awe, perhaps similar to that expressed by the psalmist. Our Scripture lesson is a praise song about the awesomeness of God. All creation cries out in praise of God.

As human beings, we can never fully comprehend the greatness of God. We can only see the evidences of God's work, the evidences of God's presence. We are marvelously created, and God has entrusted us with caring for a very special world.

Make a list of the blessings that are yours. I'm sure you will be surprised at the ways God has been at work in and through you. Give thanks to God for what you have received.

For Reflection:

What are the greatest of God's wonders?

When have you experienced an awesome moment with God?

What images would you use to describe the amazing splendor of God?

Scripture Index

("H" refers to the handout with that number.)